ISBN 3-923880-15-4

© 1983
Tetra-Press
TetraWerke Dr. rer. nat. Ulrich Baensch GmbH
D-4520 Melle 1, P.O. Box 1580, West Germany
1st edition 1976 in West Germany
5th edition 52.001–59.500, 1987
Printed in West Germany
Distributed in U.S.A. by
Tetra Sales (Division of Warner-Lambert)
Morris Plains, N.J. 07950
WL-Code: 16030

Hans A. Baensch

Marine Aquarist's Manual

**with Care and Feeding Table
for 60 Popular Tropical Marine Fish
More than 120 Color Photos**

Contents

Note

> Both U.S. and metric units have been used in this book.
> To convert litres to U.S. gallons multiply by 0.264.
> To convert °C to °F multiply by 1.8 and add 32.
> To convert centimetres (cm) to inches (ins) multiply by 0.39.

The Aquarium

Setting Up Your Aquarium

A suitable location for an aquarium can be found anywhere. Most hobbyists place the tank in the living room and that is a good idea with certain reservations. For many new to the hobby the perfect place, because of visibility, is close to the TV set, but often the most visible place in a room is not the best in terms of aquarium needs. Consider the following points:

An aquarium requires light and you can choose sunlight, artificial light or a mix. The aquarium should receive one or two hours of **morning or afternoon sun,** not more and not both. South facing windows are unsuitable since the tank can receive too much light and may become over-heated by the intensity of the midday summer sun. It is better to place the aquarium in a sunless corner since artificial light can provide most of the advantages of sunlight without the problems it can cause. The hours and intensity of electric lighting can, of course, be easily regulated.

Be sure the aquarium is placed near an electric socket. Three-pronged, earthed plugs should be used when available on all electrical equipment.

A water faucet or tap may not be close, but that is not important. You can use a bucket or hose to fill and empty the aquarium. A floor drain, sink or toilet should be within reach if very large tanks are to be kept. Any of these make it easier to change some water regularly. Synthetic carpets are an advantage since some splashing is unavoidable when cleaning aquaria. Carpets should still be covered with a plastic drip sheet when servicing the aquarium though.

Considering size, the tank should be in scale with the furnishings. When considering a marine aquarium, remember smaller tanks need more care and attention than larger ones. As a general rule use small tanks, 24 to 30 inches long (60–80 cm), for small rooms and large tanks, 40 inches (1 m) or more, for larger rooms. In either case a strong support is necessary. Your dealer has metal and wooden stands, matching all standard aquarium sizes. You can also buy units of rosewood, walnut or plastic. When choosing a unit, consider the furniture you already own. Metal stands fit everywhere. The base can be closed in to hide accessories and equipment. When setting up a large tank, more than 3 ft (1 m) long, use casters or similar supports to prevent the feet of the stand from sinking into vinyl tiles or carpets.

The new simulated wood tanks can be matched to most furniture, but if this is not possible, choose an all glass tank with white or black trim. These serve nearly every purpose. You can also design your own stand. One popular style uses a bench covered with the same carpeting as on the floor. When you build your own stand, make a rough plan just to be sure you have

Remember that tanks are very heavy when full of water. The use of casters or the like will prevent stand legs damaging soft flooring.

provided access to the aquarium equipment. The bench height should be 16–20 in (40–50 cm), adjusted to the length of the tank. To be effective an aquarium should be at least 40 in (100 cm) long and approximately 20 in (50 cm) high.

Smaller aquaria can be located on almost any short cabinet or chest, if it is solid. Remember, water is very heavy! Before filling a tank, test any home-made stand for strength. A 55 U.S. gallon (200 litre) aquarium holds 450 lbs (200 kg) of water. This added to the weight of the tank itself, gravel and accessories, can come out to approximately 675 lbs (400 kg). To duplicate that load the stand should be able to support five adults at once!

The aquarium may be built into a wall, but testing the support is more difficult. Use 2 x 4 in (5 x 10 cm) wood as supports. A 32 in (80 cm) aquarium will require six of these, reaching from the tank to the floor.

Wall installations are very popular, but there is a drawback. Such an aquarium can only be viewed from one side. "Two sided" installation is more difficult to build but very attractive.

A tastefully set-up 80 cm marine aquarium blends into, but at the same time adds to, the furnishings.

A tank up to 30 in (80 cm) in length can be built into nearly any wall. Leave room above the tank for adding or removing fish, rocks and equipment and for feeding. Equipment such as the air pump, filter, ozonizer, etc., must have a place as well. It is practical to have a cupboard beneath the tank to hide extra equipment.

The Aquarium

The question of which type of tank should be settled first; there are two types on the market suitable for use with saltwater fish and invertebrates.

Type 1: All glass with silicone-adhesive sealant.
Type 2: Plexiglas made of acrylic or, rarely, safety glass.

Experience with tanks made of other materials has not been satisfactory. Only the types mentioned have proved durable and readily available.

Freshwater aquarists who change to saltwater are advised to determine whether any tank they have satisfies requirements for use with saltwater. Iron and other metal containing aquaria are suitable only for a relatively short time, even when carefully sealed with silicone. The tanks in the table below can usually be converted to saltwater use without difficulties. Only a careful cleaning and rinsing are necessary. **Do not use detergents!** Hot water approximately 140° F (60° C) and soft towel are all that is needed.

Advantages and Disadvantages

1. All glass

Advantages:	Disadvantages:
Modern design.	Heavy.
Possibility of	The individual
do-it yourself.	panes are difficult
(Home-made tanks	to change if
never prove to be as	cracked.
accurate as	
ready-mades.)	

2. Plexiglas

Rarely break, light	Panes may be
weight, suited as	easily
quarantine or water	scratched.
supply tanks.	

Tanks with iron, brass or chrome frames are unsuitable. They may appear resistant to saltwater with a resin varnish, but even the best seal does not last forever. They can contaminate the water and cause metal poisoning in the tank inmates.

Aquarium Size

The size of the aquarium depends on the size and quantity of fish it has to house. If possible the marine aquarium should be not less than 26 gal (100 l). In larger tanks problems of evaporation and pollution by uneaten food and other organic wastes are less critical than in smaller tanks. A newcomer to the hobby should stick to this rule of thumb: **2 gal (7.5 l) of water for 1/2 in (1 cm) of fish.** Only quarantine tanks for new or diseased fishes may be stocked more heavily – but with care!

Number of Aquaria

You may ask, "Why more than one tank? I only need one aquarium." If you are typical, you will learn quickly that one aquarium will not satisfy all your needs.

Under most conditions a hobbyist places his aquarium, attractively decorated and housing his favorite fish, in the living room. When adding new fish (and every aquarist wants new fish from time to time) diseases may also be added unless all newcomers are treated in a quarantine tank before introduction into the main aquarium. On that basis alone an aquarist needs at least one additional tank which, ideally, would be the same size as the show tank. In all events it should have a capacity of at least 15 gal (60 l).

Chances are that even two aquaria will not be enough in the long run. A growing interest in marine life will make it clear for what purpose the third aquarium will be used – invertebrates such as snails, mussels, starfish, anemones and many others. These are best kept separate from fish, at least until you gain more experience in the hobby.

The Bottom Material

You can choose from several materials:
1. Coarse quartz gravel, at least 2–3 mm in size (fine quartz gravel in unsuitable).
2. Lava gravel.
3. Crushed dolomite.
4. Crushed shells.
5. Crushed corals, coral sand.
6. Combination of materials above.
7. Synthetic foam layer, covered with one of the above materials or with a combination of the above.

Other materials are not advised. Bottom materials may be omitted all together, especially in quarantine tanks. The first three materials should be carefully cleaned under running tap water to remove dust particles.

The last three materials are described in detail in the section on filtration. If you can afford it, use **crushed coral** as the substrate with a bottom filter. Crushed coral is popular both as bottom material and as a filtering material. Tiny holes and pores in

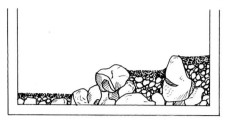

Gravel and dolomite for the substrate will usually require washing before use in the aquarium.

Careful arrangement of the rocks, coral, etc. can produce a very attractive finish.

the coral particles offer more surface area on which useful bacteria may grow.

Be sure both coral and crushed coral are free of dried organic matter. The cleaning of corals is described in the section on decoration of the aquarium (p. 18).

To determine whether the sand or crushed coral is free of organic material try this test:

1. Place the material in a plastic bucket and cover with saltwater.
2. Leave it for several days.
3. Check a sample of water with a nitrite test kit. No nitrite should be indicated.
4. Take a handful of gravel or coral from the bottom of the bucket and test for smell. There should be no hint of rotting. A foul smell indicates additional cleaning is required.

Crushed coral will usually require cleaning. Although coral sand is from the habitat of coral fish, and even though it has been bleached for more than a thousand years by the sea, the wind, and the weather, it should be checked and cleaned as described above.

How can you tell the difference between coral sand and crushed coral? There is one distinguishing feature: coral sand is rounded and ground off; crushed coral is coarse and has sharp edges.

At the front of a tank the bottom material should be one tenth as deep as the tank height. Towards the back of the tank the substratum may rise slowly. The slope guarantees a better view. Burrowing fishes may flatten the bottom and I suggest that you build a terrace-like structure with rocks beneath the sand.

Water and Its Preparation

Most hobbyists agree that it is easier to mix synthetic saltwater than to obtain natural seawater. The formula is easy: tap water + a sea salt mix = saltwater. When preparing the solution you may use water from the faucet (unless it is heavily chlorinated) and simply add a sea salt mix according to instructions. Most chemical differences in the tap water are reconciled once mixed with the salt.

There are many good salt mixes available, but do not necessarily choose the cheapest. Some mixtures may be less expensive, but some are not as pure, especially if you want to prepare a mix for the care of invertebrates.

Specific Gravity

The term "specific gravity" may be completely new, even for an experienced freshwater aquarist. It describes the "saltiness" or the amount of salt in the water.

Water density is measured with a hydrometer, an instrument as important to a marine hobbyist as a thermometer.

With the aid of a hydrometer you can easily read the specific gravity from a scale located on the thinner part of the stem which extends above the water surface.

Marine Fish, invertebrates and algae require a figure of 1.020–1.024, measured at 77°F (25°C). Be sure to use a hydrometer standardized to this temperature. Those standardized for other temperatures will not work as well when measuring the specific gravity at 77° F. The specific gravity can be raised by adding salt and can be lowered by adding freshwater.

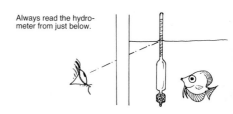

Always read the hydrometer from just below.

Check the specific gravity once every two to four weeks, according to the aquarium size. The smaller the tank, the more frequently the density needs to be checked. A 26 gal (200 l) aquarium should be checked every two to three weeks. Freshwater should be used to replace evaporated water. After each water change check the reading with the hydrometer. Evaporation can be reduced by inserting a glass plate between the lights and the water.

Salinity (ppt)

23⁰/₀₀ 24⁰/₀₀ 25⁰/₀₀ 26⁰/₀₀ 27⁰/₀₀ 28⁰/₀₀ 29⁰/₀₀ 30⁰/₀₀ 31⁰/₀₀ 32⁰/₀₀ 33⁰/₀₀ 34⁰/₀₀ 35⁰/₀₀ 36⁰/₀₀ 37⁰/₀₀ 38⁰/₀₀

TEMPERATURE — 30° C, 29° C, 28° C, 27° C, 26° C, 25° C, 24° C, 23° C, 22° C, 21° C, 20° C

SPECIFIC GRAVITY — 14, 15, 16, 17, 18, 19, 19.7, 20, 21, 22, 23, 24, 25, 26

23⁰/₀₀ 24⁰/₀₀ 25⁰/₀₀ 26⁰/₀₀ 27⁰/₀₀ 28⁰/₀₀ 29⁰/₀₀ 30⁰/₀₀ 31⁰/₀₀ 32⁰/₀₀ 33⁰/₀₀ 34⁰/₀₀ 35⁰/₀₀ 36⁰/₀₀ 37⁰/₀₀ 38⁰/₀₀

Salinity (ppt)

NB. Specific gravity figures range from 1.014 to 1.026 (see above). Prefered range is 1.020–1.024

Water Quality

Be careful when using hot water. It may have been heated in a metal-lined water heater or boiler made of copper or galvanized metal. Trace elements of soluble copper or zinc are very toxic to fish and invertebrates. In a new house with copper water pipes, be careful to check for the possibility of copper in the water system. Keep the water running for some time before using it in the aquarium. When installing new plumbing, plastic pipe is recommended, where it conforms with local building codes.

Another major concern is the water supply itself. Some water companies add chemicals to drinking water to purify it. Chlorine, for instance, is dangerous to even the toughest species. Chlorine is easily removed by the use of **AquaSafe** at the rate shown on the bottle. Tap water may also contain high nitrate levels which can be harmful to some sensitive species.

The Preparation of Saltwater

If it is your first marine aquarium, pay special attention to the quality of your tap water. The presence of chlorine is dangerous to fish, even when concentrations are low. It is always wise to de-chlorinate new water. Chlorine will disappear in the form of gas within a few hours if the water is aerated and/or filtered. Before adding fish the water should stand with aeration for one day. An alternative is the use of **AquaSafe,** a safe, simple dechlorinator.

Water, at least from the cold tap, is usually suitable for the preparation of artificial seawater. The easiest way to mix it is to put an appropriate amount of saltwater mix in a plastic container, add water and stir continuously with a wooden spoon or plastic spoon until the pail is nearly filled and the salt dissolved. Your aquarium may be filled with the resulting solution. After 80% of the tank has been filled, top up with hot water from a kettle to reach 77° F (25° C) and check its specific gravity with a hydrometer (it should read 1.020–1.024. Be sure to read the hydrometer correctly to obtain a true reading. Freshwater or strong salt water should be added while stirring continually until the correct specific gravity is obtained.

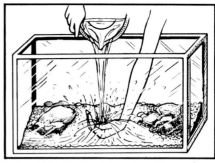
Try to avoid disturbing the substrate when adding the water

The method may seem tedious, but is recommended, especially when making partial water changes. The following is a faster way to initially fill a new aquarium with water and salt:

1. Calculate the tank's capacity.
$$\frac{\text{length x width x height}}{231}$$
= volume in U.S. gals
(To convert U.S. galls to litres, x 3.79; to Imp. gals, x 0.83.)
2. Calculate the salt mix required.
(For example, 2 bags of salt for every 20 gals of sea water.)
3. Fill the aquarium with de-chlorinated tap water.
4. The tank water should then be warmed to 77° F (25° C).
5. The salt should be added slowly, stirring continuously and with the filter running all the time.

After the temperature has been adjusted you may discover the specific gravity is too high. The reason? The bottom sand, stones and corals reduce the tank capacity. Therefore, withhold 10% of the calculated salt quantity. If the density is low it is easy to add a little more salt – but more difficult to remove it!

Naturally, fish or invertebrates cannot be added until the system has been conditioned.

Water Changes

For detailed information see the section on **Maintaining the Aquarium** (p. 83).

Something About Water Chemistry

This section is an introduction to the biological and chemical associations in your aquarium. Unfortunately, chemical processes are not always easy to explain, but I would like to try nontheless. The most important chemical terms for the saltwater aquarist are the following:
1. Ammonia (NH_3); Ammonium (NH_4^+)
2. Nitrite (NO_2)
3. Nitrate (NO_3)
4. pH-value
5. Ozone (O_3)
6. Oxygen (O_2)
7. Oxidation
8. Reduction

Ammonia, ammonium, nitrite, and nitrate are nitrogenous compounds; they are the most important and most critical combinations in natural and synthetic seawater. The life and health of your fish depends on keeping these values as low as possible. All originate from proteinaceous food remains as well as from products of metabolism (waste) of fish and other animals.

Ammonia (NH_3); Ammonium (NH_4^+)

Ammonia and ammonium cannot be measured without a good test kit. Traces as small as 0.1 ppm may be poisonous to fish. Ammonia poisoning can be avoided by good water hygiene, careful feeding, and a limited population of fish. The toxicity of ammonia is dependent on pH and temperature. The un-ionized ammonia (NH_3) becomes ionized ammonium (NH_4^+) at lower pH values. Ammonium (NH_4^+) has one more hydrogen ion thus rendering it unable to penetrate the skin of a fish, which has the protection of a membrane. NH_3, on the other hand, can penetrate the skin and is more toxic.

The nitrite level of tank is related to the amount of protein in the water. Protein is a complex of nitrogen containing compounds which enter the water through organic substances such as fish waste, excess food, and decomposing animal and plant life. It goes through a cycle of decomposition which includes ammonium/ammonia, nitrite (NO_2), and nitrate (NO_3).

The long-nosed butterfly fish, *Forcipiger flavissimus*

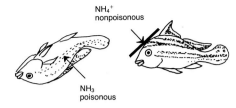

NH$_4^+$
nonpoisonous

NH$_3$
poisonous

Plants and algae take up some of the existing nitrate and ammonia ions, thus reducing the amount of nitrogen compounds in the water. When there is little oxygen in the water, nitrite is formed from excess nitrate, and when the lack of oxygen is acute, ammonium/ammonia is formed. The following table shows the effect of pH-values and temperature on the percentage of NH_3 in an ammonia/ammonium mixture.

Temperatures							
°F	72	73.5	75	77	79	81	82.5
(°C)	(22)	(23)	(24)	(25)	(26)	(27)	(28)
pH							
7.8	2.8	3.0	3.2	3.4	3.6	3.8	4.0
7.9	3.5	3.75	4.0	4.25	4.5	4.75	5.0
8.0	4.35	4.7	5.0	5.3	5.6	5.9	6.2
8.1	5.4	5.8	6.2	6.55	6.9	7.35	7.8
8.2	6.7	7.2	7.7	8.1	8.5	8.9	9.3
8.3	8.3	8.95	9.5	10.0	10.5	11.0	11.5
8.4	10.2	11.0	11.6	12.2	12.9	13.5	14.0

Fahrenheit temperatures and percentage values are rounded off.

The higher the pH the higher the NH_3. At a temperature of 77°F (25°C) and a pH of 7.8 the NH_3 proportion is 3.4% of the total. At a pH of 8.3 (which is the ideal for marines) the NH_3 is already 10%, three times as much – and three times as poisonous! It can easily and mistakenly be concluded that the pH value as well as the water temperature should be kept as low as possible. While this may seem correct in one way, it leads to other problems for marine fish.

Conversely in a freshwater aquarium ammonia/ammonium are relatively harmless (pH value 7.0–7.5) and do not cause as many difficulties. **This is one of the primary reasons why the care of freshwater fish is easier than that of a marine fish.**

Nitrite (NO$_2$)

Nitrite develops from the biological decomposition of ammonia by *Nitrosomonas* bacteria living in the filter and substrate. The nitrite value can be measured with the **TetraTest Nitrite Indicator and Colorimeter.** Values between 0.2–0.5 ppm nitrite-nitrogen are dangerous for marine fish over a period of time. Higher values will prove fatal within a few hours. Rapid breathing may be an indication that the nitrite value is too high.

After setting up a new tank, check the nitrite value daily; after approximately 10 days the nitrite value should be measured weekly. If your fish show signs of discomfort, check the nitrite value more often. The decomposition of nitrite may be achieved chemically by ozone (O$_3$). For further information on nitrite poisoning see the section on electric power failure (p. 24).

Nitrate (NO$_3$)

Nitrate values of more than 30 ppm may cause problems and even inhibit the growth of green algae. Coral polyps close when the NO$_3$ value is more than 50 ppm. For a limited time fish can tolerate values to approximately 500 ppm. Low nitrate content is important for the growth of green algae. The use of a **Tetra Nitrate Tests Kit**[*] is recommended for those having difficulties with the growth of green algae.

Nitrate in itself may not be poisonous to fish; however, the nitrate content of the water represents a constant danger. When not aerated properly, relatively non-toxic nitrate may be quickly converted into more toxic nitrite. The process is called **reduction.** A visible circulation of water, and consequently a rapid surface movement, ensure adequate aeration. An aquarium should never be so crowded that filtration failure or electric power failure can kill the fish within a short time. In a normal tank the "reserve" should last at least five to eight hours. An outside filter which has not been in action for this length of time has to be cleaned before it is switched on again.

Nitrate develops from the biological decomposition of nitrite by bacteria (*Nitrobacter)* living in the filter and substrate. Nitrifying bacteria, that is *Nitrosomonas* and *Nitrobacter,* adjust the water biologically and have a favorable influence on both NH$_3$ and NO$_2$ values. Without these useful bacteria, healthy fish would be impossible in a marine tank for an extended period of time.

Bacteria develop by themselves and can be found everywhere. Under favorable conditions their propagation in an aquarium takes place in 3–6 weeks, after which an optimum quantity has been reached. A good bottom filter and/or a large outside filter containing the proper filter material are indispensable. The development of bacteria is strongly affected, and sometimes even made impossible, by the addition of medications. Copper sulphate (CuSO$_4$), contrary to popular belief, does not destroy the bacteria in a biological filter. It may, however, reduce its effectiveness temporarily. Whenever possible, it is very important to treat diseased fish in a quarantine tank. One way to hasten the propagation of bacteria is to mix a handful of unfertilized soil with water in a pail and then add this solution to the tank water as soon as the mud has settled. A better and quicker method to obtain the necessary bacterial culture is the addition to your filter of a handful of used filter sand from the marine tank of another aquarist.

It may be safely assumed that a high nitrate value is not the only reason for the lack of growth of green algae. It is now thought that the gradual increase of nitrate levels in a tank is an indication of the concentration of other substances such as protein decomposition products. The concentration of these substances may be recognized by the yellow color of the water. By regularly changing some of the water, harmful substances as well as nitrate are removed from the tank. Partial changes of the tank water every 2–4 weeks are recommended, otherwise the aquarist should not be surprised if fatalities occur.

* Not available on a world-wide basis.

The pH-value

The average beginner does not have to pay too much attention to the pH-value as long as he or she sticks to the rules and makes regular partial water changes in the tank. Fresh seawater has a pH-stabilizing effect.

What does pH-value mean?

pH-value relates to the amount of H^+ (hydrogen) and OH^- (hydroxide) ions, expressed as a number. pH 7.0 for instance means neutral pH value (the water is neither acid nor alkaline) – the relation between H^+ and OH^- ions is equal. Saltwater fish require a pH-value of 7.8–8.3; therefore, seawater is slightly alkaline. This alkalinity is obtained by different salts, such as magnesium sulphate, and is maintained for an extended period of time by buffering. In water being used in an aquarium the pH-value sinks slowly below pH 8.0. This indicates a partial water change is needed. The lowering of the pH-value is due to the respiration of fish as well as the break down products of metabolism. An abnormal breathing rate may point to a dangerously low pH-value.

pH-Value	0 1 2 3 4 5 6 7 8 9 10 11 12 13 14
reaction	←——— acid ←— ↑ —→ alkaline ——→
	more free H^+ ions neutral more free OH-ions

Determination of the pH-value

A determination can be made with pH indicator tests kits which are easy to use (eg. **TetraTest pH High Range**).

Ozone

With the help of an ozonizer the poisonous NO_2 can be converted to NO_3. Under strong ozonization, however, the nitrite contents should be checked more frequently because ozone may become poisonous to fish as soon as the water no longer contains nitrite.

Ozone consists of three oxygen atoms (O_3). When added to the water it splits rapidly into oxygen (O_2 and O^-). This third O^- forms a compound with NO_2 (nitrite), which is oxidized to nitrate (NO_3).

NO_2	O_3	NO_3	O_2
+	=	+	
nitrite	ozone	nitrate	

Another possibility is the following; the O^- ion is unstable searches and quickly oxid-

izes tiny particles such as bacteria. The most frequent combination of the free O^- ions is with another free O^-. The normal oxygen (O_2) develops. If too much ozone is added to the tank, the skin and gills of the fish oxidize or "burn".

Oxygen (O_2) Content of the Water

The level of dissolved oxygen can be determined with an O_2 measuring instrument. In general, however, this is not necessary. Oxygen saturation occurs in a tank when there is strong aeration and low concentrations of organic waste (which devour useful oxygen). The amount of dissolved oxygen depends largely on the temperature and to a lesser extent on the specific gravity (salt content). Under increasing temperature the oxygen decreases by 10% every rise of 9° F (5° C).

The oxygen content of seawater

(expressed in mg per litre [ppm] in air saturated water).

Temperature		Specific gravity		
°F	°C	1.022	1.024	1.025
68°	20°	5.44	5.38	5.31
77°	25°	5.00	4.94	4.85
86°	30°	**4.56**	**4.50**	4.44

This demonstrates that high temperatures in a seawater tank can be harmful since the oxygen-content in healthy aquarium may be less than 5 ppm, quite a low figure.

Oxidation

Oxidation is a chemical process in which oxygen is consumed or chemically bound. For instance, the conversion from nitrite (NO_2) into nitrate (NO_3) is an oxidation process. An excess of oxygen should always exist in an aquarium for it to occur. Only in an oxygen rich environment are the *Nitrobacter* able to produce nitrate (NO_3) from nitrite (NO_2).

Reduction

Reduction is a chemical process in which oxygen is released or hydrogen is being bound. For instance, the conversion from nitrate (NO_3) into nitrite (NO_2) and then into ammonia (NH_3) are reduction processes. These can become dangerous when oxygen depletion occurs in the marine aquarium. Oxygen depletion can easily arise if the aeration fails and the supply of oxygen falls because of the respiration of the fish. Not only are the fish in danger in such a situation, but the bacteria in the substrate and in the filter cannot respire any more, nor affect oxidizing conversions. Indeed the cycle may reverse. The non-toxic nitrate may be converted to toxic nitrite. The fish suffer: they breathe quicker and may eventually die. Frequent partial water changes will keep the nitrate content low and such a danger caused by reduction will not arise.

The regular care and cleaning of the filter media is also of great importance. In a power failure, dirty media filter can produce a high nitrite concentration which will lead to the death of fish.

Trace Elements

The addition of trace elements to a marine tank has often been recommended. The author has had neither positive nor negative experiences with this procedure. However, the use of an active protein skimmer makes a regular addition of trace elements necessary (every two weeks). In a well run, balanced aquarium, with a bottom filter and regular water changes, the addition of trace elements and vitamins is not necessary. By feeding **Tetra Foods,** fish receive sufficient trace elements and vitamins in their diet.

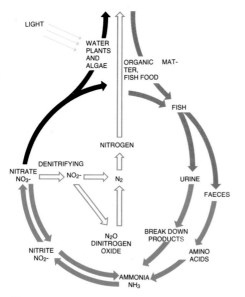

Nitrogen cycle

The nitrogen cycle in the marine aqurium. It is very important to maintain good aeration, thus encouraging the **aerobic** bacteria which convert toxic ammonia and nitrite into much less toxic nitrate. Nitrate levels are prevented from building up by regular, partial water changes.

Water Color as an Indicator

The water in a marine aquarium should always be crystal clear and transparent. The following colors can occur:

A) Whitish-Turbid

Cause: Rapid reproduction of bacteria, usually due to excessive feeding. These bacteria are dangerous, as they consume much oxygen and produce poisonous metabolic wastes. If the water smells foul, it should be completely changed at once.

Corrective Measures:
1. Use of an ultraviolet sterilizer until the turbidity has disappeared, **and/or**
2. Ozonization at about 25–30 mg/h per 26 U.S. gal (100 l) water. The appropriate quantity may be added continuously without reaching levels dangerous to fish or other animals in the aquarium, **or**
3. Water change (plus 1 and 2) **and/or**
4. Filtering through a filter into a smaller tank with the **Brilliant Super Filter and**
5. No feeding for about two to three days. Any food remains and mulm should be siphoned out.

B) Yellowish

Cause: Products of protein decomposition.

Corrective Measures: Immediate water change or a partial water change plus filtering through activated carbon.

Check: A submerged white china plate shows a yellowish appearance.

C) Greenish (Occurs very seldom, usually in warm weather only).

Cause: Mass development of unicellular algae.

Corrective Measures:
1. Copper sulphate (not be added into the show tank), **or**
2. **General Tonic.** (Attention! General Tonic together with a copper medication will cause the death of the fish!) **or**
3. Use of an ultraviolet sterilizer (Algae then "ball up" and can be removed by filtering), **or**
4. Filtering through a foam filter and strong ozonization at the same time, **or**
5. Complete change of water, **or**
6. Addition of living *Artemia* nauplii. These nauplii live on algae, **or**
7. Complete black out (no light) for at least two days together with thorough filtering, after which the filter should be cleaned.

D) Reddish

Cause: Red algae (not common).

Corrective Measure: See under C.

Cause: Side effects when a medication with antibiotics has been effected, i. e. **Tetracycline** for diseased fish.

Corrective Measure: After a disease treatment, at least $^4/_5$ of the water should be changed.

Note: antibiotics should not be added to a set-up tank.

top: brain coral with a shoal of lyretail coral fish *(Anthias squami-pinnis)*
middle: stag horn coral with the damselfish *(Abudefduf sulphur)*
bottom: organ coral *(Tubipora)*

The Decoration of The Tank

The decor of the marine tank may be constructed with various materials, such as dead coral, gravel, sandstone without metal, limestone (dolomite), marble, basalt, granite, lava bricks, slate, plastic corals etc. Unsuited are: wood, petrified wood and metallic objects.

The decor of the aquarium may simulate either a coral reef or an underwater rocky cliff. The materials may be arranged loosely or glued together. Non-toxic epoxy glues or silicone adhesives may be used for this purpose. The new aquarist would do best to only place single corals and/or single stones in his tank. Large formations are difficult to move and clean around. Single parts of the decor are easier to remove from the tank for cleaning than large, glued formations.

Stones of nearly any kind are suitable. Some sandstones (usually with a brownish appearance) contain iron in small quantities; if so, reject them. Entirely white stones, especially white quartz and marble as well as reddish lava rocks, are outstanding. This applies also to dolomite gravel. Due to the rough surface, dolomite is well suited for a marine tank. The cleaning of corals and crushed coral has been described in numerous books dealing with the marine aquarium hobby. The following is an approved method:

For one to two weeks the corals should be kept submerged in household bleach $(NaHClO_2)$ at the rate of 2 cups per gallon. After this time the corals should be soaked in freshwater for another two weeks; this water should be changed four to five times during that period.

The soaking of the corals after cleaning is absolutely necessary before they can be used in an aquarium. Corals obtained at your pet shop are generally precleaned, but if not they have to be cleaned of all organic material because it would encourage the production of ammonia and nitrite. One single coral may wipe out a whole marine tank.

The corals in your tank will become covered with algae and it is impossible to bring back the white color unless they are bleached. The aquarist should acquire two sets of coral; one set should be "at the cleaner's", while the other one is in the tank. Periodically the clean corals should be interchanged with those from the tank. (**Note:** Some aquarists prefer to let the algae grow because algae removes some harmful substances from the water.)

Because of structural features the following types of coral are suitable for use in an aquarium:

From the photos one can get an impression of the multiplicity and richness of the differing shapes and forms that corals may take. Round corals are merely attractive to the eye of the aquarist, while the branching corals offer hiding places for many fish species. These fish hide during squabbles, provoked by other fish or aggressive animals in the tank.

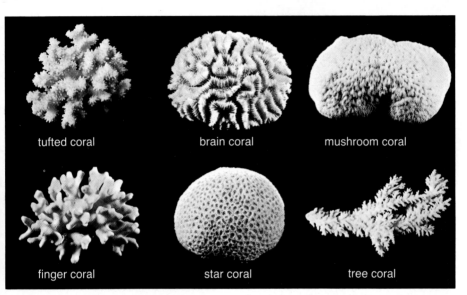

tufted coral   brain coral   mushroom coral

finger coral   star coral   tree coral

Stag Horn Corals are flat and widely branched out. Most often they are used for the decoration of the back wall. These corals should **never** be cleaned in a bleach solution, but soaked in a plastic container with fresh saltwater for a period of several weeks before placing them in an aquarium where fish have already been introduced. Before *Stag Horn Corals* are placed in the marine aquarium, the aquarist should check carefully whether they contain any remains of organic material. This is done by soaking and by measuring the nitrite value of the saltwater that has been used. *Stoney corals* are of special importance as a natural food source for quite a number of marine fish. The care and cultivation of living corals is almost impossible for the beginner. Only a few species can be kept alive in a marine tank, and then only for a few months.

When alive corals are often pink, yellowish or light blue. The white, skeleton-like image they present in a marine aquarium differs considerably from their appearance in nature. Only the beautiful red coloration of the *Organ Coral* from the Pacific Ocean remains after the soaking procedure. The organ corals contrast beautifully with white coral. *Organ coral* is so soft that the aquarist can carve holes in it with a knife, creating cavities for smaller fish to use as hiding places.

White corals can be painted with different lacquers, but the aquarist should make sure that these colors are non-toxic in the marine tank.

Algae, Marine Plants

Quite a number of plants are found in the sea. The majority are lower species such as algae. When setting up a marine tank,

A maine alga, *Caulerpa prolifera*

byist should have a quarantine tank in which to treat diseased fish.

Algal Control

In a marine tank an algae killing medication should only be employed **before** heavy growth appears, as too much decaying algae may kill your fish.

The most effective way to reduce the growth of green algae is by introducing some algae-eating fish (see page 70–74); one regal tank *(Paracanthurus hepatus)* of approximately 4 in (10 cm) will keep a tank free of filamentous algae; short algae are usually not as disturbing. Brown or blue-green algae indicate a lowering of the water quality or poor illumination. Short algae are easily removed from the glass sides with a magnet or blade scraper.

Green algae scraped from the glass sides and washed in a net can be deep frozen for

Red algae growing on a rock

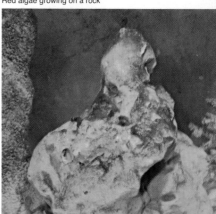

Green algae and *Caulerpa*

brown algae will initially develop on the glass sides and tank decor as well as the bottom gravel. It does not look attractive, but after a few weeks, green algae usually begin to grow. Proper lighting, however, is absolutely necessary for this to occur. The growth period of brown algae can be shortened by adding an algal stimulant to the prepared seawater. Various products are available from your dealer. Ideally, fish should not be introduced into a new marine aquarium until after green algae has started to grow.

Brownish, red, and black algae indicate poor water quality and insufficient illumination. If no green algae develop even after a water change, the period of illumination should be increased and the nitrate content and pH of the water checked.

The Death of Algae

When using medication, especially copper, the green algae are killed. They quickly decay and toxic substances are released. When algae die there is a danger fish may die also. For this reason the hob-

20

A magnificent algae growth on the reef

feeding to algae-eating fish. If the aquarist wants to encourage the growth of green algae, partial water changes should be made often to reduce harmful organic waste products.

Corals and stones may be cleaned in a bucket full of seawater with the help of a stiff brush.

A rich growth of green algae in a marine tank indicates a good water quality and only under these conditions can healthy fish life be possible. Algae should be left in a tank. They serve a useful biological purpose. To induce their growth they need fertilizing substances and different trace elements. Nitrate is produced during the biological decomposition of nitrite. It is found so abundantly in marine tanks that it often has to be removed by changing the water. Unfortunately, the water in a marine tank is usually not changed often enough. The increasing nitrate hinders the growth of algae. Green algae cannot tolerate more than 20 ppm nitrate – nitrogen (NO_3-N) for any length of time. Brown algae tolerate nitrate quantities of more than 300 ppm NO_3-N, blue-green algae approximately 150 ppm NO_3-N. An efficient protein skimmer is helpful for the healthy growth of algae. It removes the wastes before they decay.

The conditions in the tank can be determined easily from the type of algal growth:

Brown and red algae:	Bad water quality, water change necessary; illumination may be poor.
Green algae:	Good water quality; sufficient light.
Blue-green algae:	Medium water quality, dangerous to many invertebrates; tolerated by fish, excess NO_3 present.

The natural beauty of a coral reef – here in a large home aquarium!

Methods and Equipment

Filtration and Aeration

It is impossible to sustain a marine aquarium without filtration and aeration. A powerful airstone or filter that produces a vigorous surface movement of the water should be installed so the tank water will be constantly enriched with oxygen. For aeration use an air pump. Purchase a good quality unit right from the start. According to the size of the aquarium the air pump should have a capacity of 5–10 ft³ (150–300 l) per hour.

There are several kinds of filters to choose from. In this book, however, I would like to mention only the most commonly used ones:

Type 1: Bottom filter (subsand or under-gravel filter, biological filter).

Type 2: Outside filter (power filter with centrifugal pump).

Type 3: High flow filter with filter cartridge.

Type 1: Bottom Filter

A bottom filter should only be used if a quarantine tank is at the disposal of the aquarist. In an aquarium with a bottom filter one single medication can destroy the helpful bacteria. Therefore, a general rule is that **no chemical treatment be given for diseased fish in a tank with a bottom filter.** Filtration through the substrate is biological and mechanical. This filter should be combined with a Type 2 or 3 filter except in large aquaria housing a few fish ($1/2$ in fish/5 U.S. gal/1 cm fish/20 l water). Bacteria which develop in the bottom gravel convert toxic into less toxic waste products from ammonia (NH_3). The full development of a bacterial culture in the bottom substrate takes about three months. During this time the tank should contain only a few fish. The success of a good biological filter lies in the choice of an adequate substrate. Once a week the bottom should be hoovered to remove accumulated debris. Every two weeks the upper 1 in (2.5 cm) of the substrate should be stirred in order to ensure that the substrate is permeable to water. This ensures that the bacteria are supplied with oxygen. The bottom filter is operated by means of air lifts and an air pump.

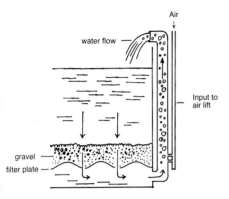

Bottom filter

With the bottom filter (as noted above), the hobbyist should also install a Type 2 or 3 filter. These filters ensure a quicker removal of all kinds of mulm (algae, food remains, etc.).

Type 2: Outside Filter

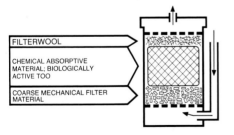

The most commonly used filter for a marine tank is an outside filter with a strong water pump. Choose a filter designed to circulate the entire volume of the tank at least once and preferably several times per hour. The circulation within the aquarium should be directed so that no places are left where mulm may gather. It may be necessary to install one or more airstones to achieve circulation. Outside filters with hose couplings require special care when joining the pipes and tubes. Adequate hose clamps are obtainable from your dealer and their use is strongly recommended.

The outside filter has to be cleaned every 1–4 months, according to the quantity of fish, the filter size and the filter material used. The filter material should always be washed in saltwater and returned to the filter so that the useful bacteria in the filter material can survive. Carbon should only be used for 8–14 days. Then is should be changed as it now contains poisonous substances that might be released back into the tank. Used filter wool should always be discarded.

Type 3: High-Flow Filter

If the marine aquarium is crowded, a high flow filter (with filter cartridge) in combination with an air pump can be used. These high flow filters, used as inside or outside filters, cannot be easily hidden so that not

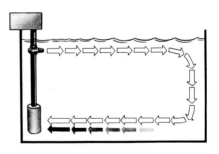

every aquarist will like them. In test, quarantine and even set-up tanks, however, these filters are very useful because of their simple and rapid cleaning method. Biological benefits cannot be obtained. It is best to clean high flow filters daily.

For the show aquarium filter Types 1 and 2 are recommended; for the quarantine tank, filter Type 3; and for built-in show tanks a combination of Type 1 and 2 or 1 and 3.

23

An outstanding filter for smaller tanks, up to 25 U.S. gal. (100 l), as well as for quarantine and holding tanks is the **Tetra Brillant Filter.** According to the water level the output of this filter is 26–65 U.S. gal/h (100–250 l/h).

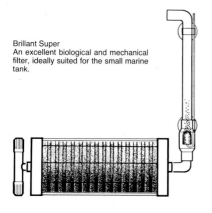

Brillant Super
An excellent biological and mechanical filter, ideally suited for the small marine tank.

Electrical Power Failure

Outside filters, and to a lesser degree bottom filters with a large amount of filter material, become dangerous when the electrical current is cut off for more than 1–2 hours. The nitrifying bacteria die from lack of oxygen. Another group of bacteria, which do not need oxygen, can change the nitrate of the tank water back to nitrite (reduction), creating a toxic condition. If the absence of water current or a non-functioning outside filter is observed by the aquarist in time (within two hours), it may safely be re-activated unless the filter is very dirty. However, if there is no circulation for a longer time the outside filter should not be started again before it is cleaned. To find out whether the water contained in the outside filter may be toxic to the animals in the marine tank, test the filter water to determine the nitrite value. If no nitrite or just a minute trace is found (up to 0.33 ppm), start the filter. However, if the nitrite value is higher than this the filter mass has to be cleaned at once in saltwater.

Aerate the marine tank especially well when the outside filter is not functioning; this is done either by an additional airstone or by the bottom filter. If the power filter is off for such a long time that nitrite is found in the tank water and the fish show discomfort, immediately change 1/3 or 1/2 of the tank water. Under these circumstances ozonization, even up to the maximum value, will not harm the fish. As usual, however, the ozonization should be stopped as soon as the nitrite content of the water has been lowered to under 0.1 ppm NO_2–N.

Sometimes water pumps will not start again after an electrical failure or after they have been switched off. It is sometimes difficult to detect that the outside filter is not working. Many aquarists place the discharge tube under the water surface in order to avoid noise. In this case, malfunction of the filter is difficult to detect. Later, the hobbyist may notice it and start the pump. Some hours later he will find his fish lying on the tank bottom, showing the typical breathing movements of nitrite poisoning. **Check the function of the filter whenever you look at your tank.** This should become a routine.

Use a bucketful of salt water to keep an external filter going during tank treatment.

If there is an acute poisoning or if some fish are dead already, the aquarist should not wait until ozone or oxygen bring the tank back to normal.

The fish should be treated as follows: A solution of seawater of normal specific gravity with the same temperature as the aquarium should be prepared in a clean bucket to which a double quantity of **AquaSafe** is added. The living fish should then be placed in the bucket with good aeration.

Usually the fish in the bucket will have recovered from their nitrite poisoning after 20 minutes. With very acute poisoning a fivefold dose of **AquaSafe** has been added and the fish may be safely placed in it.

Illumination

The daily period of illumination should be at least 12 hours. A marine tank needs a lot of light.

Lighting For Algae

The minimum wattage for algal growth may be calculated as follows:
a) 2–150 watt spot lights
   or
   2–40 watt mirror-coated fluorescent lamps (1 **Gro-Lux** and 1 soft-white or full spectrum bulb. **Gro-Lux** bulbs alone are not suitable).
   The data has been tested successfully in a 55 U.S. gal (208 l) tank 20 in (50 cm) deep.
b) A water depth of 14 in (35 cm) requires less wattage (eg. 2x100 watt spots).

Because of the heat, reflector bulbs should never be placed **in** tank covers; low voltage spot lights are also suitable but, unfortunately, are expensive when purchased with the necessary transformers. However, spot lights do add a special charm to the marine aquarium.

Invertebrates, especially anemones, like strong, even dazzling light. The best combination would be daylight coming from directly overhead and additional artificial illumination in the evening. For the care of rose corals and reef anemones, increase the light quantity mentioned by 50% to 100%. Anemones do not thrive in the light of standard incandescent lamps or poor illumination from fluorescent lamps. The aquarist should direct one spot light on an easily visible stone: anemones will rapidly assemble there.

The electrical consumption of fluorescent lamps is less than those of spot lights; they do not need frequent replacement and have the advantage of producing little additional heat. Thus, they are popular among saltwater hobbyist.

The aquarist should not economize on the amount of electricity for illumination nor on his lighting equipment. With increasing age fluorescent lamps lose their intensity and should therefore be renewed every year.

The abundant growth of algae resulting from high illumination can be controlled by algae-eating fish such as surgeons. Frequently, however, the growth of green algae does not develop due to poor illumination and only brown algae are present.

Arrange the overhead lighting to display the fish well. The light is best towards the front of the tank.

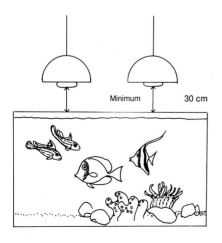

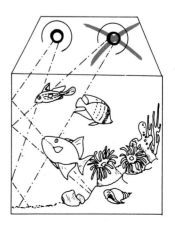

Lighting Table

Marine tanks where algal growth is desired:

Tank Depth ins (cm)	Type of lighting and intensity A or B	
	A Spotlight or diffused light, i.e. 15° Spot or 40° Flood (mirror-coated pressure lamp).	**B** Fluorescent lamps: with **Gro-Lux** and warm tone if possible.
12 (30)	1 x 60 W	at least 2 x 12 W
16 (40)	1 x 75 W	at least 2 x 15 W
20 (50)	1 x 100–150 W	at least 2 x 20 W
24 (60)	1 x 150 W⁻ 2 x 100 W	at least 3 x 20 W
28 (70)	2 x 150 W	at least 4 x 20 W

The wattage has been calculated on the basis of 16 in (40 cm) tank length; a tank of 48 in (1.20 m) length requires a threefold quantity of light. If the tanks are deeper than 20 in (50 cm), an additional lamp should be installed. Ordinary electric light bulbs are not suitable. The light source should be installed over the front third of the tank so that the colors of the fish will be illuminated from the front of the tank.

Simple rule for calculating the wattage:

Allow 5 watt per 16 in² (100 cm²) water surface area.
Of course, tanks where no algal growth is desired may be illuminated as the aquarist pleases.

Daylight

If at all possible your aquarium should be placed in a way which receives sunlight for 1–2 hours daily (morning or afternoon sun only). A crystal clear marine tank with its colorful fish life will give approximately the same impression as the diver has on a coral reef. It is possible with the help of a large mirror to reflect sunrays into the marine tank.

Temperature

The water temperature in a tropical marine aquarium should be adjusted between

The blue damselfish (Chromis cyaneus) is a hardy, beginners fish – yet still very attractive.

75–86° F (24–30° C), according to the native habitat of the fish. The minimum temperature is approximately 68° F (20° C); however, most fish rarely feed at such low temperature. Once a month the aquarist should lower the temperature to approximately 72° F (22° C) for 2–4 days by regulating the thermostatic heater. A rise in temperature promotes the metabolism and the activity of the animals in the tank; the duration of life, however, is shortened by permanent high temperatures (exceeding 82°F [28°C]). The best normal and permanent temperature lies between 75–80° F (24–27°C). In the native habitat of tropical marine fish there are only minimal temperature differences between day and night although the temperature may vary from 72–86° F (22–30° C), through different seasons of the year. **Temperatures under 68° F (20° C) and over 86° F (30° C) must be avoided.**

A natural coral reef with the green fuller (Chromis caeruleus) and the lyretail coral fish (Anthias squamipinnis).

How To Choose
Your Thermostatic Heater

All tropical marine aquaria require a good heater with an adjustable thermostat. Thermostats with a rubber seal must always be placed so that the rubber seal is about 1 ins (2.5 cm) above the water surface. The rubber seals should be checked whenever the tank is cleaned. An ideal heater for saltwater has not yet been developed. The rubber seals of any tank equipment should be given a silicone-rubber treatment to protect them against ageing. Some devices have already been equipped with silicone seals; all heaters should be checked before buying.

Electric Current in The Marine Tank

Because of poor insulation, a small electric current may get into the tank water. When this happens the aquarist will feel a fine tickle at his finger tips or forearm. Small cuts on fingers may be especially sensitive towards these currents. However, this electricity is not dangerous. Because the seawater is strongly conductive, it will blow a fuse or breaker switch before you get seriously hurt. Nevertheless, you should be careful with electrical connections around the marine aquarium.

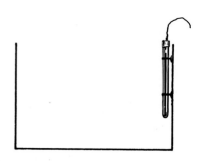

Summer or in heated rooms:
2 watts per U.S. gallon (about 1 watt per 2 litres)

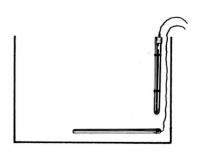

Winter or in unheated rooms:
4 watts per U.S. gallon (or 1–2 watts per litre)

When handling the electrical equipment, the power supply plug should always be disconnected. Handle electric plugs with special care after you have been working in the marine tank. Always use a dry towel.

Heating

The heater's output should be calculated the same way as in freshwater tanks; in summer and in heated rooms, 2 watts per U.S. gallon of water; in unheated rooms and in winter, 4 watts per U.S. gallon of water.

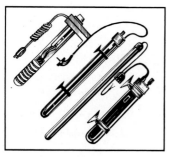

Heater – thermostats

Tank Volume and Heater Wattage

Tank Volume	Warm Room – Wattage of the Thermostatic Heaters	Cool Room – Wattage of the Thermostatic Heaters
13 gal (50 l)	25 Watt	50 Watt
20 gal (75 l)	50 Watt	75 Watt
26 gal (100 l)	50 Watt	100 Watt
40 gal (150 l)	75 Watt	150 Watt
55 gal (200 l)	100 Watt	200 Watt
80 gal (300 l)	150 Watt	300 Watt
130 gal (500 l)	250 Watt	500 Watt

The tank temperature may reach more than 86° F (30° C) in summer. On such hot days protect the room against direct sun with the help of blinds or curtains. The sides of the tank can also be covered with aluminium foil. The best insulation is obtained by glueng thin styrofoam plates around the tank. During the day the front glass can be covered as well. Artificial light may be also responsible for too much heat. For safety's sake **switch off the lighting on hot summer days.**

Good aeration is vital in the marine aquarium.

Do not allow the water temperature to get over 86° F (30° C). The oxygen content is strongly reduced in warm water, thus causing the fish to die of oxygen difficultes. Accordingly, strong aeration is essential on hot summer days. The tank may be cooled by hanging plastic containers with ice cubes in the tank. Do not forget to siphon off a corresponding quantity of water before placing the container into the aquarium to avoid an overflow.

Failure of the heater on cold days and the resulting lowering of the temperature is quickly indicated by the fish. They do not eat; it is useless to feed them because this will only foul the water. Bring the temperature slowly back to normal values of between 75–79° F (24–26° C). If the heater is defective and it is impossible to replace it (on weekends, for example), the hobbyist should warm up the aquarium by hanging non-metal buckets or other containers filled with hot water in the tank.

Do not use electric immersion-heaters in the marine tank. They heat the water much too quickly and uncontrollably; your fish might even get burned. It is better to siphon off ¼ to ½ of the tank contents into a plastic tub where an immersion-heater may warm it up to 104–122° F (40–50° C). After reaching this temperature the water should be slowly poured into the tank. The aquarist should pay attention to the fact that cooling down or warming up too rapidly may be harmful to fish.

The tank temperature has to be checked daily. Put the back of your hand on the front glass of the tank while reading the temperature. Your will get a feeling over a period of time for the right temperature in case the thermometer should be misplaced or broken. Use a **Tetra** liquid crystal thermometer which fixes to the outside of the aquarium – not too near the heater though. Some thermometers may deviate up to 9° F (5° C) which may be very dangerous to the life of your fish. Mercury thermometers should never enter an aquarium. If they get broken the mercury will poison the fish. If a tank contains a large trigger fish or angelfish, it is a good idea to cover the thermometer with a plastic tube as these fish like to bite floating thermometers into little pieces!

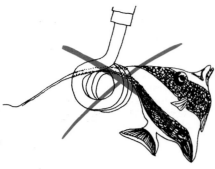

Avoid the use of electric immersion heaters such as this in the marine aqurium.

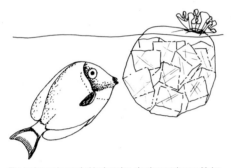

The tank may be cooled by hanging plastic containers with ice cubes in the tank.

Tetra Liquid Crystal Thermometer.

Protein Skimmer, Ozone, and Ultraviolet Light

The use of a protein skimmer in marine tanks is very popular in Germany. This is not the case in other countries. Is a protein skimmer necessary or not? This question cannot be answered easily. I would recommend the following: tanks with only a few fish, especially if there is a biological filter, do not require a protein skimmer. The same is true for tanks with a strong growth of green algae. Other tanks **will** need a protein skimmer. There are different types of protein skimmers with differing effectiveness:

Type 1: Simple glued plastic tubes. Usually the output is not satisfactory.
Type 2: Contact skimmer or countercurrent skimmer. This type uses air mixed with ozone and is not easy to adjust; a strong air pump and good air valves are indispensable. Apart from its difficult adjustment, this protein skimmer is effective and practical, especially pricewise. To raise the efficiency it should be run with both ozone and air.
Type 3: High-powered skimmers with a strong pump are recommended for aquaria over 65 gal (250 l) containing many fish.

The above mentioned protein skimmers are able to remove proteinaceous remains before they become toxic to the fish and invertebrates. My personal experiences with the various skimmers has been good. One single careless feeding may foul the water. A protein skimmer helps prevent this.

Negatively charged ozone ions decompose the positively charged protein molecules in the skimmer. The protein coagulates and can thus be skimmed off. The hard foam of protein is poisonous and should not enter the tank again. The skimmer pot has to be emptied daily.

The ozonizer is just as useful as the protein skimmer. Tanks which contain only a few

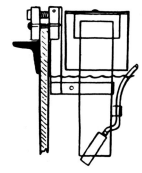

Two different types of protein skimmer. This type of apperatus is not essential for all tanks but is useful in some situations.

If the hobbyist can restrain himself from overcrowding his tank (approximately 5 in [13 cm] of fish for 26 U.S. gal [100 l] water), he can do without a protein skimmer or an ozonizer. More crowded tanks need both devices, bearing in mind that the protein skimmer is the more important.

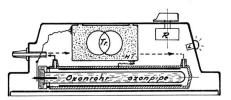

An ozonizer – another useful but not essential piece of equipment.

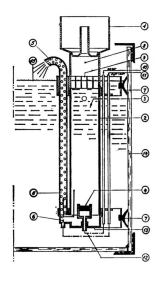

Dosage of Ozone

Ozone is produced by high voltage (60,000 V) in the contact tube of the ozonizer. If inhaled in large quantities, it can be toxic and may lead to headaches or dizziness. Adjust the ozonizer in such a way that hardly any smell of ozone can be detected in the room.

In general, fish tolerate up to 25 mg ozone (O_3) per 50 gal (200 l) of water per hour. The quantitiy of ozone released should be adjusted with the control dial on the equipment. By far the largest amount of ozone is reduced to oxygen (O_2) in the tank water. If too much O_3 is added to the tank continuously it may prove harmful to your fish; it can burn skin and gills.

Ultraviolet Rays

The bacteria-killing effect of ultraviolet rays is well known. The killing of bacteria can also be accomplished with ozone. The aquarist who possesses an ozonizer does not need an ultraviolet lamp. The hobbyist who buys an ultraviolet lamp because it is less expensive than the ozonizer should know that the ultraviolet bulb has a life of 3000–4000 hours. Although the bulb continues to shine, the quartz glass does not allow the ultraviolet rays to come through. This, however, cannot be seen. In view of the fact that an ultraviolet lamp should always be switched on, its lifetime is approximately three to six months.

fish do not require an ozonizer; tanks with many fish profit from one. By ozonizing, the aquarist obtains a nearly sterile marine tank where the development of harmful bacteria is hardly possible. A sterile tank may run perfectly for a certain amount of time, but biological stability cannot be obtained. So use with care!

Three ultraviolet bulbs, however, cost approximately as much as an ozonizer does. If the hobbyist relies on an ultraviolet lamp and wants to install one, it is best to do so on the outside of the tank to avoid the fish getting hurt by the rays. Otherwise, the directions for use should always be followed. Ultraviolet rays will never lead to damage, even when used continuously, as long as they do not get directly into the tank where they may harm the fish. Caution: **You should never look at a germicidal U.V. lamp unless it is shielded by water or eye damage may result.**

UV-Steriliser

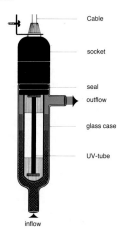

- Cable
- socket
- seal
- outflow
- glass case
- UV-tube

inflow

Setting Up A Saltwater Aquarium

1. Install first a bottom filter (subsand filter). (Omit this step in the quarantine tank).
2. Wash the substrate material and place in the tank. (Omit this step in a quarantine tank). The best suited bottom materials are crushed coral, crushed shells, dolomite gravel (for the balancing of pH-value), and quartz gravel, 3–5 mm in size. Fine sand should be used only in aquaria without bottom filters and then only in very thin layers. Crushed coral and coral sand have to

be checked carefully to be certain they are free of organic material.

3. Install thermostatic heater to maintain a temperature of 75–80° F (24–27° C). The output of the heater should be calculated carefully: 4 watts per U.S. gal (1 watt per l) in unheated rooms: 2 watts per U.S. gal (1 watt per 2 l) in well heated rooms.
4. Install an outside or inside filter; outside filter for a show tank, with at least 50 U.S. gal/hr (200 l/hr) capacity; inside filter such as a high flow filter for larger quarantine tanks. For quarantine tanks or show tanks up to 40 U.S. gal (150 l) use a **Tetra Brillant Super Filter.**
5. Additional aeration by airstones is only necessary if the filtration system is not effective enough. An air pump, however, is still necessary for operation of the bottom filter. Choose a sufficiently strong pump with an output of at least 10 ft^3 (300 l) per hour. If the air pump is installed below the water surface level, place a check valve between the pump and tank. This will avoid back-siphoning of water and possible damage to the pump if electricity is shut off.
6. Protein skimmer, ozonizer or an ultraviolet lamp can be installed if needed.
7. Arrange tank decorations (i. e. dolomite chunks, or corals). Stones that contain metal are not suitable. Try to hide the technical equipment with the decorative material.
8. Add saltwater with a specific density of 1.022–1.024. For control purposes use a hydrometer standardized for 75–77° F (24–25° C).

top: a beautiful shoal wimple fish, *Heniochus,* in their Red Sea home.

bottom: a shoal of marine catfish *(Plotosus).*

32

9. Install the light fixture. At least a 40 watt fluorescent light is required for every 16 in (40 cm) length in a 20 in (50 cm) deep aquarium. **Use 1 watt per cm length of the tank as a guide.** If the aquarist installs more than one fluorescent lamp it is recommended he chooses one in white or "warmtone" to use with a **Gro-Lux** lamp. Mirror-coated fluorescent lamps are more efficient because they produce a higher light output. Spot lights and pressure lamps are excellent. If these kinds of lamps are used, the wattage would be at least double that used with fluorescent lamps.

10. If possible, the tank should be left to stand for 2–3 weeks before introducing the fish. Within this period, however, the filter and heating units should be kept switched on. After this, algae covered stones and a small quantity of substrate from the tanks of friends can be added to promote the colonization of useful micro-organisms.

11. Add the fish (over a period of weeks), not to the aquarium but to the quarantine tank first. Most marine fish have diseases which have to be treated before the fish are placed in the show tank. New fish should be observed for 2–3 weeks to determine if they are healthy.

12. Use cover glasses, cut into shape by a glazier. Leave space for cords as well as filter tubes and pipes. Cover glasses are indispensable: they stop fish from jumping out, prevent heat loss and reduce evaporation.

Introducing the Fish

You will usually bring the fish home in a plastic bag. Float this container in the tank for 5–10 minutes. After opening the plastic bag, one third of the contents should be emptied into a bucket; the bag is then refilled with the same amount of water taken from the tank. This acclimation procedure should be repeated after 5 minutes. This enables your fish to adapt themselves to their new environment. Now they may be released into the quarantine tank. If there is no quarantine tank, the newcomers should be introduced into the show tank after the

normal dose of **MarinOomed*** (or similar treatment) has been added. **MarinOomed** should be added again after three days to prevent infections and any outbreak of disease.

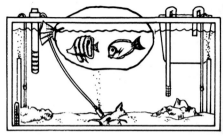

Float new fish in their plastic bag before releasing them. This will allow the temperature to equalise and prevent temperature shock.

First Feeding

It is advisable not to feed the fish until they have adapted themselves to their new environment and are swimming briskly around. If they hide in corners or hover, showing pale colors, quite possibly something is wrong.

Is the temperature correct?
Was the water too fresh? (Not if **Aqua-Safe** has been added).
Are lighting and substrate colors too bright? Do the decorations offer enough hiding places for the fish? Are the fish healthy? (Or do they show little white spots on fins and body?)

It is best to feed your fish sparingly during the first few weeks. Too much food will quickly foul the water.

Two feedings per day are sufficient. The portions given should be eaten by the fish completely within one minute. After 3–4 weeks the aquarist may feed 3–4 times a day as by now the fish are biologically established and useful bacteria have developed in the tank. With their help metabolic wastes are rendered harmless and the aquarium water is closer to a natural state. The aquarist who has time and likes to watch his fish can feed them small portions until they are satisfied. This is easily recognized because they are not as active as they were at the beginning of the feeding.

***Note:** not available on a worldwide basis.

The Fish

Their Collection and Importation

Of the more than 1 million living creatures that are known to man, we (as aquarists) are interested in the fish. Their number is estimated at 25,000 species, but only those suited for the novice marine aquarist are mentioned here. There are many more species suitable for tank life than are listed below. The species pictured and described have been chosen in view of their availability and ease of care.

Of course, the possibility of obtaining certain fish species differs geographically. For instance, it is much easier in the U.S. to obtain fish from the Caribbean or the coast of Florida than it is in Europe. Nearby collection areas as well as favorable connections to international airports are of definite importance to the trade. However, in both Europe and the U.S. most fish dealers offer coral fish from all over the world at reasonable prices. Unlike tropical freshwater fish, tropical marine fish are not easily kept in tanks; and, except for a few species, they do not reproduce in aquaria. As a result they are more expensive than most tropical freshwater fish.

Nearly every marine fish in your dealer's tank or your own has been caught in the wild, which means that a few days or weeks ago it was collected from its native habitat, put in a plastic bag filled with water and oxygen, and shipped from Sri Lanka, Manila, Singapore, Georgetown or Miami. This journey often takes 18–36 hours and, apart from temperature changes, the fish suffer from a decrease in the oxygen content of the water as well as lack of space during transport. They are not fed. As a consequence the fish may lose weight and suffer from internal disturbances. It is not unusual for fish to refuse to eat new kinds of food in their aquarium surroundings. Losses are inevitable with delicate species. Newly imported marines frequently suffer from diseases which develop more easily in weakened fish. You will read more about this in the section on disease.

Does this sound like a gloomy view of the collection and maintenance of tropical marine fish? Yes, and with good reason! The beauty of many many coral fish tempts unexperienced hobbyists to buy them. Roughly speaking, 25% of all marine fish survive no more than 8 weeks after they have been caught. Some die in the collector's holding tanks, others during transport. Still others die at the importers' and in pet shops. Most of them, however, die sooner or later in the tanks of the aquarist. All those involved in collection and importation have experience in the treatment of newly collected marine fish, at least one assumes so. A new marine hobbyist, however, does not.

In terms of conservation, every hobbyist should be aware of the fact that his buying of rare coral fish may deprive coral reefs all over the world of their inhabitants. The author does not want to exaggerate or condemn the hobby of keeping coral reef fish in general; he would just like to mention the problems and ask the aquarist to restrict himself in the beginning to fish that are relatively hardy. Many such species have a high reproductive capacity and can easily replace those caught for aquaria if they are collected sensibly.

It is in areas like this that marine coral fish abound.

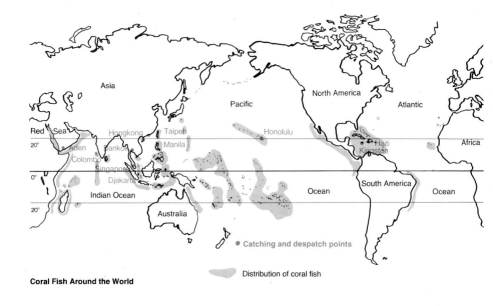

Coral Fish Around the World

Distribution of coral fish

● Catching and despatch points

Fish Names, Characteristics and Identification

The systematic classification of marine fish changes constantly, as does all scientific work. With the help and assistance of Dr. Terofal of the Zoologische Staatssammlung of Munich and Prof. Dr. Ladiges of Hamburg, the author has tried to use upto-date names. The fish pictures correspond with the data in the table. Even when the aquarist knows another name for a fish, he should use the name mentioned underneath the picture when reading the Care and Feeding Table. All fish species mentioned in this table have been kept by the author. The data, especially those in the feeding plan, have been proven correct.

The identification of a particular fish may cause great difficulties. The origin of the scientific classification system goes back to the Swedish scientist Linnaeus. In 1758 he published his **Systema Naturae,** stating the basic ideas of systematic classification.

Fish, like other animals, are divided as follows:

Class: . . . .
Order: . . . .
Superorder: . . . .
Family: . . . .
Genus: . . . .
Species: . . . .

The **genus** is always written before the **species** and is written with a capital letter. The second word stands for the species and does not start with a capital. If there is another Latin word following, which does not have a capital, it stands for the subspecies. Usually, the name of the scientist who first described the fish follows the species name; the name of the scientist may again be followed by a date indicating the year the fish was first described.

The hobbyist has to know something about the anatomy of the fish if he wants to identify it. The number of fins and their structure play an important role in the classification of fish (fin formula). A dorsal fin may show different forms: short or high, long-

36

stretched or divided. In some species the soft posterior part of the dorsal fin acts as a means of locomotion when slow movements are made. The front dorsal spines of some fish are so hard and pointed that they are used as weapons.

In a few cases the first dorsal spines contain channels and glands and their puncture is venomous. If this happens to a human being, the consequence may be an itching allergy and strong swelling, blood poisoning or even death. Of the species mentioned in the table only the lion fish, *Pterois volitans,* and the coral catfish, *Plotosus anguillaris,* are dangerous, but hardly fatal.

If in spite of all caution one of the species mentioned or other species should injure a human being and great pain is felt, seek medical help immediately. The author was stung by a fox face, *Lo vulpinus,* a frequently imported species, in the ball of his hand. The pain became so intense and the swelling was so great that within 15 minutes medical attention was necessary. At the hospital an anti-allergic drug and a strong sedative had to be injected. Be careful when handling specimens with dorsal spines! Never catch these fish with your hand. Never try to seize one of these fish when it is struggling in the net.

To avoid injury to either the aquarist or his fish, they should be caught in a glass jar or a transparent plastic container, with the help of one or two nets. One fish at a time is driven into the container, the opening is then closed with the net and the container is removed from the tank. With part of the water the fish should be poured into the transport container. Be careful the fish does not jump out!

Another feature of the fish's anatomy is the preopercular and the opercular bones (gill covers). Some fish groups, such as the angelfish have one or more sharp spines on the bottom of the gill covers which can be used as a weapon when the covers are opened. Some fish species have a serrated edge on the gill cover, others a rounded-off one. These characteristics are of importance for the identification of the different fish families. One distinguishing characteristic, for example, when comparing *Abudefduf* and *Pomacentrus* is that *Abudefduf* has a rounded-off gill cover and *Pomacentrus* has a serrated one. On a photo this usually cannot be seen and it is necessary to put one fish at the disposal of an ichthyologist to enable him to determine the species. In addition, he needs to know the locality where the fish was collected. Another important factor is the mouth and

Fish Identification – some salient points using the tigerfish *(Therapon jarbua).*

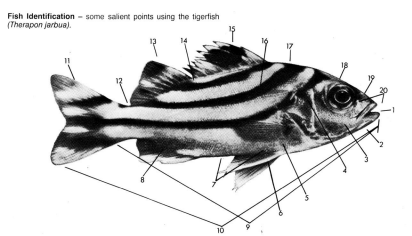

1. Mouth – 2. Chin – 3. Cheek – 4. Gill cover – 5. Chest – 6. Pelvic fins – 7. Pectoral fins – 8. Anal fin – 9. Standard length – 10. Fork length – 11. Caudal (tail) fin – 12. Peduncle – 13. Hind dorsal fin – 14. Back – 15. Front dorsal fin – 16. Flank and lateral line – 17. Neck – 18. Head – 19. Snout – 20. Nostrils.

its differences in form and placement, as well as the adaptations for food intake. From these characteristics the aquarist may learn, whether it is predatory or perhaps a coral-eating fish. Triggerfish, angelfish, trunk fish and parrot fish have a "beak" and are able to crack shells and coral branches. Fish that live on small animals have small mouths which enable them to eat animal plankton. In a tank these fish species have to be fed frequently because they are not able to accept large quantities of food in one feeding. Some species, such as the long-nosed butterfly, have a long, tweezer-like mouth. With their elongated jaws they can pick small food

The fox face (Lo vulpinus)

such as worms, snails and coral polyps even from tiny cracks.

The lateral line, straight in some species and wave-like in others, sometimes in one line and sometimes divided, is the most important sense organ of the fish besides the eye. It serves as an sensor for pressure and sounds. With the help of the lateral line the fish is able to recognize the slightest changes in its surroundings.

Carefully chase a fish into a glass beaker.

Seahorses are very delicate feeders, often requiring live brine shrimp. They are best kept in a tank with no other fish.

Fish that are armed with hard dorsal spines, strong teeth, sharp spines on the gill plates, or (as surgeons) sharp spikes on the caudal fin, should be released into the community tank with caution and their behavior towards other tank inhabitants carefully checked. Fish without such weapons are usually harmless, feeding on small animals or plants and usually hiding from enemies or swimming away. These fish should be offered coral branches, etc. in the tank so they may retreat if a situation becomes threatening. Such species are nearly always well suited for the community tank. Quite a number of harmless looking damsel fish are so quarrelsome that they do not allow smaller fish (even of their own kind) to eat. Here, also, the aquarist has to provide sufficient hiding places.

Suggested Combinations of Fish By Tank Volume

A) Not more than 1 in (2.5 cm) of fish for every 5 U.S. gal U (20 l) of tank water.

$$\frac{\text{tank volume in gallons}}{5}$$

= fish capacity in inches,

or $\dfrac{\text{tank volume in litres}}{2.5 \times 20}$

= fish capacity in cm

N.B. Deduct 10 % of total tank volume to allow for gravel, rocks, etc.

By Filter Surface Area

B) 0.4 in (1 cm) of fish for every 24 in^2 (150 cm^2) filter surface area.
or
1 in fish length for 60 in^2 filter surface

Examples of Fish Combinations in a Marine Tank

Tank length 30 in (80 cm), contents 26 gal (100 l).

1.	2 *Amphiprion ocellaris*	3 in
	at 1 in (3 cm)	(9 cm)
	1 *Amphiprion sebae*	1.5 in
		(4 cm)
		Total 4.5 in
		(13 cm)
2.	1 *Heniochus acuminatus*	3 in
		(8 cm)
	2 *Amphiprion ocellaris*	2 in
	at 1 in (3 cm)	(6 cm)
		Total 5 in
		(14 cm)
3.	1 *Abudefduf oxyodon*	1.5 in
		(4 cm)
	1 *Abudefduf sulphur*	1 in
		(3 cm)
	2 *Dascyllus aruanus*	2 in
	at 1 in (3 cm)	(6 cm)
		Total 4.5 in
		(13 cm)

Suggestions for a tank of 48 in (120 cm) and approximately 70 gal (270 l) contents.

4.	3 *Pomacentrus melanochir*	3 in
	at 3 in (2.5 cm)	(7.5 cm)
	1 *Chaetodon lunula*	2 in
	at 2 in (6 cm)	(6.0 cm)

	3 *Amphiprion frenatus* or	
	Amphiprion ephippium	4.5 in
	at 1.5 in (4 cm)	(12 cm)
	1 *Acanthurus leucosternon*	4.5 in
		(12 cm)
		Total 14 in
		(37.5 cm)
5.	1 *Coris* at 2.5 in (7 cm)	2.5 in
		(7.0 cm)
	3 *Amphiprion ocellaris*	3.5 in
	at 3.5 cm	(10.5 cm)
	2 *Chaetodon vagabundus*	5 in
	at 2.5 in (6 cm)	(12.0 cm)
	1 *Paracanthurus hepatus*	3 in
		(7.0 cm)
		Total 14 in
		(36.5 cm)
6.	1 *Amphiprion frenatus*	1.5 in
		(4.0 cm)
	5 *Amphiprion ocellaris*	5 in
	at 1 in (3 cm)	(15.0 cm)
	2 *Amphiprion clarkii* or	3 in
	Amphiprion sebae 1.5 in	(8.0 cm)
	1 *Heniochus acuminatus*	3.5 in
		(10.0 cm)
		Total 13 in
		(37.0 cm)

Only when a filter system is working properly are the above suggested combinations possible. Crushed shells or curshed coral on the tank bottom should be at least 2.5 ins (6 cm) thick (approximately 2–5 mm in size). Fish should never be overfed.
The bottom filter should have a water flow of at least 1 gal/h/76 in^2 (1 l/h/20 cm^2) gravel surface (i.e. the bottom filter with 640 in^2 [4000 cm^2] bottom surface should have an output of 52 gal/h [200 l/h]). Newly installed tanks should never house more fish than the above mentioned rule allows. Later, when the bottom filter is working properly, 1 in (2.5 cm) of fish for 3.5 U.S. gal (13 l) of tank water is permitted.
It then follows that the aquarist should start with a few hardy species; after 2–3 months he may buy other, less robust ones. These, however, should first be put into the quarantine tank, where they should be observed (and treated) for 2–3 weeks. When releasing fish into the show tank for the first time, the aquarist should remember that

juvenile fish will grow when properly fed. After some months of careful feeding a 1 in (2.5 cm) specimen could have attained a length of 2 in (5 cm). This is especially true for most species of damsels. Other species may not grow as rapidly as this, but the aquarist should consider some increase in length when calculating his stocking level.

Invertebrates

Except for snails and unwelcome guests such as *Hydra* there are few invertebrates to be found in freshwater tanks. For a marine aquarium, however, there is a varied assortment at hand: crabs, shrimps, starfish, snails, mussels, living corals, worms, and, last but not least, anemones. Unfortunately, it is impossible to keep them all together in an aquarium. The aquarist should make it a principle to never keep fish and invertebrates together. This is especially true for the new hobbyist.

The novice should stick to this rule, especially if he owns only one tank and does not possess a holding tank for diseased fish or a quarantine tank, as recommended earlier. Invertebrates are easily killed with the commonly used medications, especially copper sulphate. An exception is **MarinOomed** from **Tetra.**

Of course, if your pet hermit crab or anemone is in a tank with diseased fish, it should be removed from the aquarium and put into another tank or, if none is at hand, into a bucket. This may do well for 1–2 days or until treatment of the aquarium is completed.

There are some hardy invertebrates such as starfish that can be kept together with certain fish species. These animals are not described in this book because the new marine aquarist is usually only interested in colorful fish at first.

The author would like to mention that there is a special charm about a tank where invertebrates and fish are kept together, as for instance anemones with clownfish *(Amphiprion).* These combinations, however, have to be left to the advanced hobbyist. The aquarist must be well acquainted with his fish if he wants to set up a community tank with invertebrates **and** fish. It will take time and attention to study their requirements and behavior in a community set-up.

A beautifully set-up marine tank

A diver feeding *Anthias* out of his hands (Red sea)

A Selection Of Beautiful And Hardy Saltwater Fish

A special color section in this book has been dedicated to a selection of fish species. Details concerning their care and maintenance can easily be found in the *Care and Feeding Table.* There are no detailed descriptions of the fish as the photos will sufficiently show their richness in color and form. Only those characteristics that could not be included in the *Care and Feeding Table* are mentioned in this section. The photos show fish that are commonly available. In some cases juvenile forms are shown. It is indicated whether a juvenile or adult is pictured; some marine fish look different when young and change with age. Light, water conditions, day and night coloration play an important role in the appearance of the fish. Care has been taken to show the fish in their "normal" coloration: they are healthy and the photos were taken during the day.

Damselfish *(Pomacentridae)*

*Abudefduf, Amphiprion, Chromis,
Dascyllus, Eupomacentrus, Pomacentrus*

This family has many species. The majority of them are ideally suited for aquarium life due to their small size and hardy nature. Their native habitats are tropical and subtropical oceans. Most varieties adapt well to varying water conditions, which makes them especially suitable for the new aquarist. However, since they dominate weaker fish of their own kind as well as other tank mates, the aquarist requires a certain knowledge of compatible fish combinations (p. 39). It is best, therefore, to buy specimens of approximately the same size and to provide sufficient hiding places in the tank. With few exceptions, most members of this family accept flake food readily. When fed 4–5 times a day these fish can live **exclusively** on this diet. During a vacation all the species in this family can be maintained with a good automatic feeding device.

Cloudy damsels *(Dascyllus carneus)*
between the coral in their native marine home

1
Blue Damsel
Abudefduf (assimilis) cyaneus
Though quarrelsome towards its own kind, it usually takes kindly to other fish. Likes small holes as hiding places, suited for small community tanks; hardy variety.

2
Neon Damsel
Abudefduf oxyodon
As *A. cyaneus;* requires, however, a larger aquarium as it grows bigger. Its dorsal spines can cause painful injuries if the aquarist is careless.

3
Sergeant Major
Abudefduf saxatilis
A hardy, peaceful fish. Less bossy than other varieties of the same family; grows larger than most damsels.

4
Yellow Damsel
Abudefduf sulphur
Well-suited for the community tank, more delicate than other varieties; frequent water changes are recommended. Likes plenty of hiding places.

43

5
Maroon Clown
   Amphiprion biaculeatus
   (formerly *Premnas biaculeatus*)
Sensitive to poor water quality (nitrite/nitrate). Same needs and requirements as other clownfish; aggressive to its close relatives. Also known as the spike-cheeked clown.

6
Yellow-Tailed Clown
   Amphiprion clarkii
   (formerly A. xanthurus)
This variety with its 2–3 vertical white bars often shows yellow-black colored pectoral, anal, and caudal fins. One of the hardiest species in the saltwater aquarium.

7
Cardinal Clown
   Amphiprion ephippium
Should only be kept singly in the community tank; quarrelsome towards its own kind. Does not require a particular species of sea anemone. No white collar encircling the after part of the head; dark dorsal stain.

8
Tomato Clown
   Amphiprion frenatus
Behavior and requirements similar to *A. ephippium*. White collar encircling the after part of head. Juvenile specimens have two bands. *A. frenatus* is often described as *A. melanopus*. According to Schulz, however, *A. melanopus* is a black-red variety of *A. frenatus*.

8a
Tomato Clown
Amphiprion frenatus
Another color variety, lacking the
shading on the flanks. Possibly a
young specimen.

9
Clown Anemone Fish
Amphiprion ocellaris
(formerly *A. percula*)
Most popular marine fish, easy to
maintain with good water conditions.
Does not require a sea anemone.
Should be fed 5 times a day at least.
If color fading occurs **General Tonic**
plus **AquaSafe** should be used.

10
Skunk Clown
Amphiprion perideraion
A white band covers its gill plates.
Peaceful, but more delicate than oth-
er clownfish. Needs an anemone
more than the above species.

11
Saddle-Back Clown
Amphiprion polymnus
More delicate than the above species. Irresistible due to its peculiar
way of swimming. Together with an
anemone and gentle companions it
will show its best appearance.

45

12
Orange Skunk Clown
Amphiprion sandaracinos
(formerly *A. akallopisos*)
Appearance and requirements similar to *A. perideraion,* but without the white band on its gill plates.

13
Yellow-Tailed Clown
Amphiprion sebae
Very variable form, depending where collected in its range – it may be just a variant of *A. clarkii* (see above). Hardy, peaceful, suitable for the community tank. Hearty eater, hiding morsels; when feeding the aquarist has to watch that all food has been eaten.

14
Green Chromis
Chromis caeruleus
Peaceful shoaling fish; needs plenty of hiding places (coral), frequent feedings and tiny morsels. Loves fresh saltwater. Good-natured; single specimens are often shy.

15
Yellow-Tailed Damsel
Chromis xanthurus
Easy to keep shoaling fish even in tanks under 30 in (75 cm); however, bossy towards its own kind. Name disputed. Klausewitz describes this fish as *Abudefduf parasema;* Frank de Graaf calls it *Pomacentrus caeruleus.* A scientific revision of these names is certainly needed.

46

16
Three-Striped Damsel, Humbug
  Dascyllus aruanus
Easy to keep. Single specimens or
pairs are suitable for the community
aquarium. Spawns if kept properly;
rearing of young, however, very difficult.

17
Reticulated Damsel, Cloudy Damsel
  Dascyllus carneus
Not as hardy as *D. aruanus*. Needs
hiding places. Belligerent towards
fish of its own family – otherwise
does well in a community tank.

18
Striped Damsel Fish
  Dascyllus marginatus
This fish is especially belligerent.
Usually it tolerates only a few other
Dascyllus species in the same tank.
Has to be offered good hiding places.
Seems to tolerate *Amphiprion* spe-
cies. Seems to prefer warmer tank
water than other species of this fami-
ly. Otherwise, it does very well in the
marine aquarium.

19
Four-Striped Damsel,
Black Tailed Humbug
  Dascyllus melanurus
Like *D. aruanus,* showing 4 vertical
black bars.

47

20
Three-Spotted Damselfish,
Domino Damsel
  Dascyllus trimaculatus
Hardy, belligerent species, adult form not as charming as the juvenile. All kinds of food accepted, even takes it away from other fish. Although suitable for the beginner, it may become aggressive when grown-up.

21
Beau Gregory
  Eupomacentrus leucostictus
A common damsel from the Caribbean, suitable for the community tank. All fish of this family are very hardy. Needs hiding places.

top:
Amphiprion ocellaris in its anemone

22
Blue-Finned Damsel
  Pomacentrus melanochir
Maintenance and care same as blue damsel in this table. Native habitat: Indian Ocean. Belligerent towards fish of his own kind, and fish species which resemble it. Therefore, only fish of approximately same size as *P. melanochir* are suited as tank mates.

23
Yellow-Bellied Damsel
  Pomacentrus pavo
Maintenance and care as mentioned above. Native habitat: Sri Lanka. Not as belligerent as *P. melanochir*. Axelrod describes this fish as *Pomacentrus pulcherrimus*.

bottom:
Amphiprion in an anemone

48

Butterfly Fish

The name "butterfly fish" applies especially well to this family. Any diver who has watched these jewels of the sea on a coral reef will confirm this. They live in pairs, or, according to species, in shoals. In the Caribbean we find only a few species and their colors are not very vivid. However, there are many different species in the Indian and Pacific Oceans. Butterfly fish are seldom shy. Before they flee from an intruder, they erect their dorsal rays for defense. Only weak specimens hide when threatened.

Butterfly fish may be choosy feeders. Some species eat only one variety of coral polyp and these will not be mentioned further as they are rarely imported and probably would not survive in a marine aquarium. However, the specimens described in this book prove to be very hardy when accustomed to aquarium life, although they require very good water conditions. A regular weekly check of the nitrite value as well as a checking of the nitrate content every two weeks are necessary. If possible, these fish should only be kept in a well established tank with a rich growth of green algae. They require frequent partial water changes.

22

22
Threadfin Butterfly
Chaetodon auriga
One of the hardiest butterfly fish easily adapting itself to aquarium life. Not suitable for a community tank with other aggressive species.

23
Red-Tail Butterfly, Brown Butterfly
Chaetodon collare
Difficult to feed at first but, after a period of acclimation, it is rather easy to keep. Peaceful, likes hiding places.

23

24
Black Back Butterfly
Chaetodon melannotus
Not as colorful as the above mentioned species. Requires very fine food. Otherwise kept as other butterfly fish; juvenile specimens are rather sensitive.

50

25
Pearlscale Butterfly
Chaetodon xanturus
After a difficult period of adaptation
this fish will do well in a tank if the
aquarist provides good water conditions and a variety of foods. Social
and most of the time peaceful. Likes
warmth; sensitive to injuries.

26
Racoon Butterfly, Moon Butterfly
Chaetodon lunula
One of the hardiest species among
butterfly fish; peaceful and enduring.

27
Yellow Butterfly
Chaetodon semilarvatus
Beautiful schooling species. Likes
fish of its own kind. After adaptation it
becomes rather tame. Dry food is only accepted when *C. semilarvatus*
has been accustomed to it when it
was young. Not a species for the new
hobbyist. Needs a large tank of 40 in
(1 m) length or more.

28
Vagabond Butterfly
Chaetodon vagabundus
Hardiest butterfly fish. No special requirements regarding food. Well suited for the community tank. Smaller specimens, however, need a period of adaptation until dry food are accepted.

28a
Indian Ocean Butterfly,
Eight Banded Butterfly
Chaetodon decussatus
(formerly *C. pictus*)
Often described as a subspecies of *C. vagabundus*. It is, however, a separate species. Maintenance and feeding as *C. vagabundus*.

29
Copper-Banded Butterfly
Chelmon rostratus
A delicate species, choosy regarding its food. Will die if not fed properly (usually accepts only small shrimps and worms). Requires extremely clear water; a fish for the experienced hobbyist only.

30
Long-Nosed Butterfly
Forciper flavissimus
As *Chelmon rostratus,* but not as choosy regarding its food. After a period of adaptation accepts flake food and even takes it out of the aquarist's hand.

52

31
Banner Fish, Royal Coachman
Heniochus acuminatus
A decorative species which is easy to keep in nearly every tank. Very suitable for the community tank. Occasionally belligerent towards fish of its own kind. Accepts all kinds of food. *Heniochus acuminatus* is the hardiest specimen of the entire family. A group of three is very pleasant, as they are easily fed and, due to their behavior, add a special charm to any large marine aquarium. As with other marine fish, they cannot tolerate dirty water or even the slightest pollution.

Angelfish

32
Queen Angelfish
Holocanthus ciliaris
(Angelichthys ciliaris)

A. ciliaris becomes tame rapidly and accepts food morsels from its owners' hands. The aquarist should take a half or a quarter **TetraTip** between his fingers and move it to and fro in the water; by doing this *A. ciliaris* is conditioned to dry food. Don't be afraid; this fish does not bite and even takes the food very carefully from your fingers. **TetraTips** have so many nourishing ingredients that *A. ciliaris* can be kept alive for years when fed this food. As with all angelfish, *A. ciliaris* has a very stout gill spine. The aquarist must be careful not to get hurt when catching this fish; it is advisable to use a glass or plastic container.

53

33
Pygmy Angel
Centropyge argi
A small charming fish, suitable as a tank mate for more delicate species. Not choosy in regard to food but requires good water conditions. Likes small holes as hiding places and frequent but small feedings.

34
Bi-Color Angel
Centropyge bicolor
A magnificent brilliant fish but difficult and not a species for the new aquarist. Suited as companion for more delicate species; requires hiding places.

35
Rock Beauty
Holocanthus tricolor
(juvenile and adult)
A very delicate fish species, maintained only under excellent water and feeding conditions. *H. tricolor* should only be bought by the experienced aquarist who has a well balanced large tank at his disposal. It should never be associated with hearty eaters and hardy species because it will not get enough food.

Holacanthus tricolor (adult)

Right:
Emperor angelfish *(Pomacanthus imperator)*

54

Pomacanthus Angelfish

These fish have earned the name "angel" fish because of their graceful movements and beautiful colors. Specimens should be kept singly, at least after a length of 4 in (10 cm) has been reached. Otherwise, they will constantly fight and it will be difficult for the weaker fish to get food at all. Juvenile forms differ in coloration from adults. They are hardy fish that may grow to a ripe old age if the aquarist provides excellent tank water, attentive care and varied food. Juvenile specimens are especially susceptible to diseases and starvation-two days without nourishment and they can grow thin and become even more susceptible to disease. If they have not accepted food for one week, it is unlikely there is any possibility of saving them from starvation; when purchasing them the aquarist should make sure that they are accepting food.

36
Emperor Angel
Pomacanthus imperator
As all angelfish, *P. imperator* lives
singly. Suitable for large community
tanks of 75 gal (300 l) or more. After a
period of adaptation accepts food out
of the owner's hands. (Illustrated top
left, juvenile fish.)

37
French Angel
Pomacanthus paru
Rather hardy species. Juvenile fish
are black with yellow bands; mature
fish turn grey. Should be maintained
as all angelfish. (Illustrated centre
left, juvenile fish.)

38
Koran Angel
Pomacanthus semicirculatus
Juvenile specimens have a very interesting appearance, later they
have a simpler pattern. Susceptible
to diseases; after a period of adaptation, however, a fairly hardy species.
A fish for the community tank, hostile
only towards fish of its own kind. (Illustrated bottom left, juvenile fish.)

57

Surgeon Fish (Tangs)

These fish get the name "surgeon fish" from the scalpel-like, thorn-shaped pair of spines found at the base of the tail. These spines, which protrude in case of danger, can inflict injuries to other fish. It is therefore not advisable to keep several large specimens together in one tank. After the difficult period of acclimation to tank life has been overcome, surgeons are hardy. They accept any kind of food but prefer algae. Frequent feedings are necessary as surgeon fish do not swallow large morsels in one bite, but are always searching for food while swimming. Although belligerent and even dangerous to their own kind in the aquarium, they live in large schools in their native habitat.

39
Blue Tang
Acanthurus coeruleus
The juvenile form is yellow (see top left); later yellow-blue-grey coloration with yellow anal fin changing to a gorgeous sky-blue. As all surgeon fish, it is belligerent towards its own kind, otherwise tolerant. An algae-eater. (Juvenile form above left, adult form left.)

40
Powder-Blue Surgeon Fish
Acanthurus leucosternon
One of the most beautiful marine fish. A rather hardy species, belligerent towards other blue-colored fish. Should be introduced only after remaining tank inhabitants have established themselves. With its good appetite, A. leucosternon is a pleasure to keep. Algae based foods absolutely necessary: **TetraMarin Large Flakes** should be fed frequently.

58

41
Yellow-Tailed Blue Tang,
Regal Tang
Paracanthurus hepatus
A surgeon fish that will remain rather
small. Kept singly or with other species, *P. hepatus* is a delightful tank
inhabitant and has beautiful colors.
Algae are preferred as a main diet,
supplemented by **Tetra Conditioning Food** and **TetraMarin.** With 4–5
feedings per day this surgeon fish will
thrive. Also known as "the bluest
thing on earth". Very susceptible to
infestation with *Oodinium.* More frequent treatments necessary than
with other marine fish.

42
Purple Tang
Zebrasoma xanthurum
If the aquarist wants this surgeon fish
to thrive, abundant rich algae growth
is indispensable. *Z. xanthurum* requires similar care to *Paracanthurus
hepatus,* but is sometimes more vi-
cious.

Various Families
43
Sharp-Nosed Puffer
Canthigaster valenti
Not a fish for the novice aquarist because it sometimes inflicts injuries by
nipping the fins of its tank mates.
Otherwise a hardy fish. Family: *Can-
thigasteridae.*

59

44
Coris formosa
   (Juvenile form left;
   adult form below)
Its interesting coloration and pleasant behavior make this fish very
popular. It hides in the bottom sand at
night and requires fine sand or at
least a sandy corner.
Family: *Labridae.*

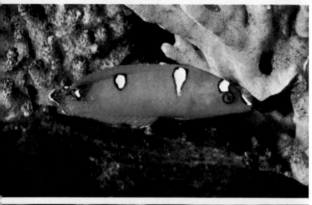

Coris formosa (adult)

45
Clown Wrasse
   Coris gaimard
   (juvenile form left)
Family: *Labridae.*

Coris gaimard (adult)

60

45b
Yellow Wrasse
Thalassoma lutescens
Care and maintenance as for above *Coris* species. *T. lutescens,* however, is not as delicate as these *Coris* species. No special requirements with regard to feeding but prefers frozen food. Family: *Labridae.*

46
Neon Goby
Elacatinus oceanops
Small, amusing fish, requiring fine live food: accepts **Tetra-FD-Menu** as well. Its habit of "cleaning" larger fish makes *E. oceanops* especially interesting. Unfortunately, it is very susceptible to poor water conditions. Family: *Gobiidae.*

47
Royal Gramma
Gramma loreto
Sometimes choosy about its food, otherwise a beautiful little fish, especially suited for the aquarist with a lot of time. Very attractive, likes hiding places. Family: *Grammidae.*

48
Squirrel Fish
Holocentrus rubrum
Shy, greedy fish, darting in and out of holes, as it likes darkness. Snatches up floating food morsels **(TetraTips).** Peaceful, but delicate. Needs a lot of oxygen. Family: *Holocentridae.*

61

49
Cleaner Wrasse
Labroides dimidiatus
Should never be absent from any large tank with tank mates of 4 in (10 cm) and larger: unselfishly "cleans" smaller tank inhabitants, too. Peaceful but not very easily kept. Should not be mistaken as *Aspidontis,* a predatory fish. Family: *Labridae.*

50
Long-Horned Cowfish
Lactoria cornuta
Fascinating fish, becomes tame enough to accept food from its owner's hands. Peaceful but not easily kept. Family: *Ostraciontidae.*

51
Mono or Fingerfish
Monodactylus argenteus
Can be kept in freshwater as well as in saltwater, where it becomes more beautiful. It is a glutton and will accept every kind of food. Social fish, easily adapted to aquarium feeding. Helps other species to acclimate. Too hardy for smaller, delicate fish; tireless swimmer. Family: *Monodactylidae.*

52
Big-eye Soldierfish
Myripristis murdjan
Not easily adapted to tank life as with all fish of this family. Suitable for the experienced aquarist with a large tank offering hiding places. Should be fed nourishing food. Attractive due to the brilliant red color, contrasting beautifully with other aquarium habitants. Unfortunately, *M. murdjan* is shy and prefers to follow a shy, quiet life. Family: *Holocentridae.*

Right picture: Squirrel fish live in schools, preferably under umbrella-shaped corals, protecting them against enemies from above.

62

53
Red-Toothed Triggerfish
Odonus niger
Requires nourishing food which should be hardshelled in order to blunt its teeth, which grow very rapidly. Family: *Balistidae*.

54
Round Batfish
Platax orbicularis
Charming juvenile form, becomes a very large if fed abundantly. For very large show tanks only, otherwise it will soon outgrow the aquarium. Becomes peaceful and tame very quickly. Family: *Platacidae*.

55
Coral Catfish
Plotosus anguillaris
Poisonous! Its dorsal fin rays are venomous, even for humans. Be careful when handling this fish! Easily kept, peaceful, accepts nearly all kinds of food. Likes hiding places; shy when kept singly. Family: *Plotosidae*.

56
Humu-Humu-Nuku-Nuku-A-Puaa, Picasso Trigger
Rhinecanthus aculeatus
All new aquarists love smaller specimens of *R. aculeatus*. It turns its eyes while searching for anything that might be edible. Strangely, flake food is seldom accepted. Rather peaceful fish in a community tank. Family: *Balistidae*.

57
Lionfish
Pterois volitans
Poisonous! Its dorsal fin spines are very poisonous. Not a fish for the new aquarist. To be fed exclusively on living fish (e. g. guppies or goldfish) at the outset. Completely unsuitable for the community tank with smaller fish. Otherwise easily kept and very attractive. In the long run, however, its behavior is rather boring. A predatory fish, always on the look-out for a meal! Family: *Scorpaenidae*.

58
Scat
Scatophagus argus
Behavior like *Monodactylus argenteus; S. argus,* however, becomes very tame. A glutton. Susceptible to disease, but most parasites will die off when exposed to freshwater to which this fish will adapt within 2–3 days. Therefore, a durable fish for the new aquarist. Family: *Scatophagidae*.

65

Ruby Scat
Scatophagus argus rubrifrons
This subspecies is less frequently imported and not as easily kept. Mentioned here because of its attractiveness. Family: *Scatophagidae.*

59
Bluehead Wrasse
Thalassoma bifasciatum
A quick, agile swimmer, requiring a tank of 40 in (1 m) length or more. Accepts nearly every kind of food; frequent feedings necessary. Belligerent towards its own kind. Juveniles and females show a yellow color with a vertical band in the middle of the body. Illustration shows a male. Hides in the sand at night just as *Coris* species do; therefore, a sandy corner is indispensable. Family: *Labridae.*

60
Moorish Idol
Zanclus canescens
This very delicate algae-eater, after a period of adaptation, accepts flake food from its owner's fingers. Fish that refuse to eat may be exposed to freshwater for 20 minutes, after which they should be offered algae. Very attractive after adaptation to tank life. Family: *Zanclidae.*

Care and Maintenance

The Feeding of Your Fish

The feeding of most marine fish is just as easy as the feeding of freshwater fish. However, if the aquarist wants his fish to grow, he has to feed them more frequently and with a more nourishing diet because the majority of marine fish grow larger than most freshwater fish. An exception to this rule are the damsel fish. These species are more readily maintained with dry foods than species that grow larger.

Until now a disappointing growth rate for marine fish was attributed to the exclusive use diet of dry foods and their poor quality. The discoveries of new research as well as practical results obtained in the **Tetra Marine Department** proved that many marine fish may be maintained entirely on dry foods such as **TetraMin** or **TetraMarin.** The food quantity, however, has to be adjusted according to the requirements of each fish.

TetraMarin, a dry food especially for marine fish, was used when working out a comprehensive feeding table for 60 of the most popular saltwater fish. The results are based on practical experience of several well known marine aquarists, including the author. Special thanks are due to **Mr. Peter Chlupaty** for his co-operation on the feeding table. In this book suggestions with regard to feeding may be obtained from the feeding plan and the chart.

The healthy appetite of saltwater fish makes every feed a special pleasure for the hobbyist. Fish take food flakes or other foods right out of their owner's fingers. This promotes an intimate contact between the aquarist and his fish which helps to maintain an interest in the aquarium and its life. Descriptions of the different foods necessary for saltwater fish are given in connection with the table. The quantity of food as well as the frequency of feeding depend to a large extent on the particular species.

How To Feed Your Fish

1. Never shake the food directly from the drum into the tank. Take the portion to be fed between thumb and forefinger and dip this quantity just below the water surface; few marine fish take their food from the water surface. (For most marine fish **TetraMarin Large Flakes** recommended.)

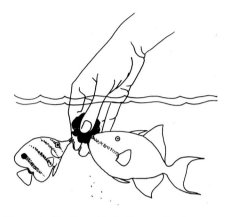

Many marine fish will soon take food from your hand.

2. When feeding, the filter and aeration should be cut down to avoid flakes being swirled into a corner where fish might not reach them.

3. Just a tiny feed should be offered to determine whether the fish are hungry or not. Something may be wrong if they do not rush to eat the food immediately.

4. Fish should receive only one full feeding a day. This **main** feeding may take from 2–10 minutes. The remaining 2–4 feedings should consist of a very small amount of dry food or **TetraTips.**

5. The aquarist has to make sure that every fish gets some food and the special requirements of particular fish species have to be considered.

6. A community tank of fish with the same feeding requirements is an advantage for the novice aquarist. But even a newcomer to this hobby should be able to keep fish with differing food requirements together in the same tank, i. e. *Dascyllus, Amphiprion,* and *Chromis* (eating flake food) and groupers (living on tablet food).

7. Shy fish not wanting to leave their hiding places should be offered food on a little stick or the food may be placed before their hiding places with the aid of a plastic tube. If they still do not accept food they must be removed to a separate tank where the hobbyist can try to acclimate them to dry foods or some other food. Generally, frozen brine shrimp should be offered first or some shrimp and clam meat can be put on a piece of coral and dried before being offered.

8. If fish refuse to eat, they should be observed closely. Perhaps a symptom of illness can be spotted. If this is not the case the aquarist should check and see that some established, easy-to-feed fish are in the tank. This arouses the feeding response in newcomers and they become adapted to dry foods as well as to their new surroundings. In case this little trick does not help, the aquarist is referred to point 7 above. A good candidate for the acclimation of new fish is *Scatophagus argus,* as it accepts any kind of food very tamely after only a few days, even from the hand of the aquarist. Other fish frequently join them when they feed.

9. One day per week no food should be offered. Only very young fish, less than 1 in (2.5 cm) in length should be exempt from this rule.

10. Frozen food should be thawed out before feeding, especially for those fish which swallow whole pieces. Frozen brine shrimp, however, does not need to be thawed as small fish nibble them off as they float on the surface. This feeding method avoids entire morsels sinking to the bottom of the tank without being noticed by the aquarist.

11. Feeding living worms *(Tubifex,* enchytraeids and grindal worms) may prove to be dangerous if this food sinks to the bottom of the tank without being eaten immediately. These animals can burrow quickly into the sand. *Tubifex* decay after a few minutes and enchytraeids after two days and may foul the water.

12. Uneaten food must be removed at once, especially when using earthworms, pieces of mussels, clams or pieces of fish. Uneaten pieces may be removed with a siphon tube.

Often more aggressive eaters catch all the food and leave nothing for the more delicate species. Even good natured fish can become rowdy when it comes to feeding. In such a case the aquarist has to decide to remove one of the fish and put it into a different tank.

The following is one example of how to acclimate fish during a period of adaptation: A large tank is divided by means of a glass partition. Newcomers or delicate fish remain in one half, stronger specimens in the other. Then small portions of clams, scallops and shrimp may be offered to the delicate fish. The inhabitants of the other half of the tank are fed **TetraMarin Large Flakes** or shrimp or anything they are used to being fed.

Removal of uneaten food morsels using a stiff piece of plastic. Removal of your thumb after the tube has been placed in the water will cause nearby food items to be drawn in. Replacement of your thumb allows the tube with its contents to be removed from the tank.

Abudefduf saxatilis (Sergeant Major)

Chaetodon xanthurus (Pearl-scale Butterflyfish)

The glass partition allows the fish to see and get used to each other. The aquarist may try removing it after 1–2 weeks. A glass partition will temporaily solve the problem between aggressive and delicate eaters in a community tank. After a longer period of adaptation, the more delicate fish will help themselves just as eagerly as the rest at feeding time. They lose their shyness because hunger forces them to, they may even become so tame that they adapt to hand-feeding. This allows the aquarist to check the feeding very closely while hearty eaters are fed in a different corner of the tank.

The hobbyist who wants to feed the easy way, if he does not have the time for procuring and preparing special foods, should only choose fish species that are easily maintained with readily accessible foods.

Due to the change from complicated feeding methods (such as mussels, etc.) to easy to handle flake and tablet foods, the saltwater hobby certainly will make considerable progress. Forty of the 60 species mentioned in the Care and Feeding Table can live entirely on **Tetra** foods. This allows even the new aquarist a rich choice of beautiful fish for his first saltwater aquarium.

Delayed treatment of diseases and overfeeding are the most frequent reasons for failures in a marine aquarium. Therefore, it is recommended that the aquarist pay special attention to the following suggestions. If he has already been successful with the care and maintenance of freshwater fish it is likely that he has a good eye for correct feeding.

Small fish (up to 1.5 in [3.75 cm] in length) require small quantities but frequently, at least 5 times daily. Two of these feedings should consist of brine shrimp. Larger specimens do not require more than three feeds daily. Large predatory fish (lionfish, for example) should be fed only 2–3 times a week.

Once a day the aquarist should take time off and ensure that his fish are fed until they are **really** satisfied. It is not always easy to obtain live food such as brine shrimp *(Artemia)* or worms and it is possible that they may not be obtainable at all. The author has, therefore, paid special attention to indicate a reliable diet for the fish mentioned in the Care and Feeding Table using the extensive food range from **Tetra.**

Care and Feeding Table

for the successful care of 60 of the more popular marine fishes

Tetra

by Hans Baensch

Family	#	Scientific Name / Popular Name	Amount of Care Required	Native Habitat	Compatibility	Avg. Size Adult (in/cm)	Min. Tank Length (in/cm)	TetraMarin, TetraMin	Tetra Cond. Food / Algae, Lettuce	Tetra FD-Menü / FD-Food fd FD	TetraTips	Frozen Food, Fresh Food FF	Artemia / Livefood
Pomacentridae – Damselfishes	1	Abudefduf cyaneus / Fiji Devil, Blue Reef Fish	回	Pac. Ind.	✕	2 / 6	28 / 70	T		fd ••		F	A
	2	Abudefduf oxyodon / Neon Damsel	回	Pac. Ind.	✕	3 / 8	32 / 80	T	⊘	FD	⌇	F	
	3	Abudefduf saxatilis / Sergeant Major	☐	Pac. Ind. R.S. Car.	✕	5 / 12	32 / 80	T	⊘ ⊘	fd		F	
	4	Abudefduf sulphur / Yellow Damselfish, Sulphur Damselfish	回	Ind.	✕	3 / 8	28 / 70	T		FD ••		F	A
	5	Amphiprion biaculeatus / Maroon Clownfish	回	Pac.		3-4 / 9	32 / 80	T		FD		F	A
	6	Amphiprion clarkii / Yellow-tailed Clownfish	☐	Pac. Ind.	✕	4 / 10	32 / 80	T	⊘ ⊘	fd	⌇		
	7	Amphiprion ephippium / Cardinal Clownfish	回	Pac. Ind.		3 / 8	28 / 70	T		FD ••		F	A
	8	Amphiprion frenatus / Tomato Clownfish	回	Pac. Ind.		5 / 14	32 / 80	T		FD ••		F	A
	9	Amphiprion ocellaris / Common Clownfish	☐	Ind.	✕	3 / 7	28 / 70	T		fd ••		F	A
	10	Amphiprion perideraion / Skunk Clownfish	◼	Pac. Ind.	✕	2 / 5	28 / 70	T		FD ••		F	A
	11	Amphiprion polymnus / Saddle-Back Clownfish	◼	Pac. Ind.	✕	5 / 12	32 / 80	T		FD ••	⟅	F	A
	12	Amphiprion sandaracinos / Orange Skunk Clownfish	◼	Pac. Ind.	✕	2 / 6	28 / 70	T		FD ••		F	A
	13	Amphiprion sebae / Yellowtail Clownfish	☐	Pac. Ind.		3-4 / 9	32 / 80	T	⊘	fd ••	⟋		A
	14	Chromis caeruleus / Green Damselfish	回	Ind. R.S.	✕	3 / 8	32 / 80	T		fd ••		F	A
	15	Chromis xanthurus / Yellow tail	☐	Pac. Ind.	✕	4 / 10	32 / 80	T	⊘	fd ••	⌣	F	A
	16	Dascyllus aruanus / Humbug	☐	Ind. R.S.	✕	2-3 / 7	24 / 60	T	⊘	fd ••	⟅		A
	17	Dascyllus carneus / Cloudy Damselfish	回	Pac. Ind.	✕	3 / 7	28 / 70	T	⊘	fd ••	⟅		A
	18	Dascyllus marginatus / Striped Damselfish	回	Ind. R.S.	✕	2 / 5	28 / 70	T	⊘	fd ••			A
	19	Dascyllus melanurus / Black-tailed Dascyllus	☐	Pac.	✕	3 / 7	28 / 70	T	⊘	fd ••	⟅		A
	20	Dascyllus trimaculatus / Domino-Damselfish	☐	Pac. Ind. R.S.	✕	5 / 12	32 / 80	T		fd ••			A
	21	Eupomacentrus leucostictus / Beau Gregory	回	Car.	✕	6 / 15	28 / 70	T	⊘	fd ••			

70

Explanation to the Table

Amount of Care Required

☐ These fish are easy to keep and are in general well-suited for the community tank. Easy to maintain with **Tetra** flake foods, as mentioned in the table under "Feeding Plan".

▣ These fish are easy to keep, too. More attention, however, must be given to the water quality. The water has to be changed regularly, otherwise skin diseases may occur. pH-value, nitrite, and nitrate content of the water have to be checked regularly.

▦ These fish are not suited for beginners, great attention must be given to which foods they will eat. At least one third of their food has to be live food or an equivalent, unless otherwise stated in the Feeding Table that a dry food may be given as basic diet. In this case, occasional feedings (1–2 times a week) of live (or frozen food as a substitute) are sufficient. Absolutely necessary for a successful care once again is the regular changing of the tank water. Apart from that, an attentive, careful feeding, which will take 10–20 minutes twice a week, will be a contribution to the successful keeping of fish.

■ Not suited for the beginner. In most cases only conditionally suitable for the community tank. Sensitive with regard to medication, for instance copper, except **MarinOomed,** and/or requiring special food so that at least two years of successful experience with regard to the keeping of salt-water fish are required in order to care for these species. In some cases so-called "algae tanks" ease the keeping of these species or make it possible at all.

🌐 Native Habitat

The tropical fish mentioned in the "Care and Feeding Table" are well-suited for the community tank. Apart from very few exceptions (Red Sea, or lagoons, where sometimes rivers mix with sea-water) the composition of the surface waters of all oceans all over the world is alike. The tolerance of salt-water fishes with regard to the density makes it possible to recommend an average value for the majority of them. Apart from that it is not easy to know the exact area from which the fish comes.

The Care and Feeding Table explains how to successfully keep fish of different species in one tank. Fish that are easy to keep

Significance of the Abbreviations:	Average Density at 25° C (77° F)	Average Salt Content ‰	Temperatures in Degrees ° C (° F)
1. Pac. = Pacific Ocean, Indopacific (especially Philippines, Indonesia, Malaysia up to Thailand, Singapore)	1.021	32	22–28 (72–82)
2. Ind. = Indian Ocean (Ceylon, East-African Coast, also Seychelles, Mauritius)	1.023	34	20–22 (68–72)
3. R.S. = Red Sea	1.027	40	20–30 (68–86)
4. Car. = Caribbean Sea – Atlantic Ocean (tropical Atlantic, especially Caribbean Sea, Bahamas, Florida)	1.024	35	20–28 (68–82)

Threadfin Butterflyfish   Moon Butterflyfish

Family		Scientific Name / Popular Name	Amount of Care Required	Native Habitat: Pac., Ind., R.S., Car.	Compatibility	Average Size of Adult Fish inch./cm	Minimum Tank Length inch./cm	TetraMarin, TetraMin (T) — 1	Tetra Conditioning Food, Algae Al Al, Lettuce Let — 2-3	Tetra FD-Menü, FD-Food fd FD — 4-5	TetraTips — 6	Frozen Food, Fresh Food F — 7-8	Artemia A A / Livefood L L — 9-10
Chaetodontidae subfamily Chaetodontinae Butterflyfishes	22	Chaetodon auriga / Threadfin Butterflyfish	▣	Pac. Ind. R.S.		6 / 15	40 / 100	T	⌀	FD	⌙	F	A
	23	Chaetodon xanthurus / Pearl-scale Butterflyfish	▣	Ind. R.S.	⋈	5 / 12	32 / 80	**T**	⌀	FD		F	A
	24	Chaetodon collare / Brown Butterflyfish	▪	Pac. Ind.		5 / 12	32 / 80	T	Al			F	A
	25	Chaetodon lunula / Moon Butterflyfish	▣	Pac. Ind. R.S.	⋈	6 / 16	40 / 100	T	⊘		⌙	F	A
	26	Chaetodon melannotus / Black-backed Butterflyfish	▣	Ind. R.S.	⋈	5 / 12	32 / 80	**T**	⊘ Al			F	A
	27	Chaetodon semilarvatus / Yellow Butterflyfish	▣	R.S.	⋈	6 / 15	40 / 100	T		FD		F	
	28	Chaetodon vagabundus / Vagabond Butterflyfish	▣	Ind. R.S.	⋈	6 / 16	40 / 100	**T**	⊘	FD		F	A
	29	Chelmon rostratus / Copperbanded Butterflyfish	▪	Pac. Ind.	⋖	5 / 12	32 / 80			FD		F	A
	30	Forcipiger flavissimus / Longnosed Butterflyfish	▪	Pac. Ind.	⋖	6 / 15	40 / 100	T		FD		F	A L
	31	Heniochus acuminatus / Bannerfish	▣	Pac. Ind.		8 / 20	40 / 100	**T**	⌀ ⊘ Al	fd		F	A
Chaetodontidae subfamily Pomacanthinae Angelfishes	32	Holocanthus ciliaris / Queen Angelfish	▪	Car.	◂	12 / 30	48 / 120	T	⊘	FD	▬	F	
	33	Centropyge argi / Pygmy Angelfish	▣	Car.		2 / 5	28 / 70	**T**	⌀ Al	FD ••	▭	F	A
	34	Centropyge bicolor / Two-colored Angelfish	▪	Pac. Ind.	⋈	4 / 10	32 / 80	T		FD		F	A L
	35	Holacanthus tricolor / Rock Beauty	▪	Car.		12 / 30	40 / 100	T	Al	FD	⟋	F	A L
	36	Pomacanthus imperator / Emperor Angelfish	▪	Pac. Ind. R.S. Car.		12 / 30	48 / 120	T	⊘ Al Let	FD	⟋	F	L
	37	Pomacanthus paru / French Angelfish	▣	Car.	◂	10 / 25	40 / 100	T	⊘	FD	▭	F	L
	38	Pomacanthus semicirculatus / Koran Angelfish	▣	Pac. Ind. R.S.	◂	12 / 30	48 / 120	T	⊘ Al Let	FD		F	L
Acanthuridae Surgeonfishes	39	Acanthurus coeruleus / Blue Tang	▣	Car.	◂	8 / 20	32 / 80	**T**	⊘ Al Let	FD ••	⌙	F	
	40	Acanthurus leucosternon / Powder-blue Surgeonfish	▣	Pac. Ind.	◂	8 / 20	48 / 100	**T**	⊘ Al Let	FD	⌙	F	
	41	Paracanthurus hepatus / Regal Tang	▣	Pac. Ind.	◂	7 / 18	32 / 80	**T**	⊘ Al Let	FD ••		F	A
	42	Zebrasoma xanthurum / Purple Surgeonfish	▣	Pac. Ind.	◂	9-10 / 24	48 / 100	T	◉	FD	▭	F	

bear the sign □ or and are well-suited for the community tank even if they have a different native habitat. If these species can be kept together according to the column headed "compatibility" they are well-suited for the community tank with regard to water density and temperature.

Compatibility

This column shows how many fish of one species the aquarist can possibly keep together in a community tank or species tank.

◁ = Single Fish

Unless you have a really large tank, you should keep only one fish of this species. Keeping more than one would result in constant fighting, which in some cases might even result in the death of the weaker fish. However, these fish are generally hostile toward other species and they can usually be kept in a community tank.

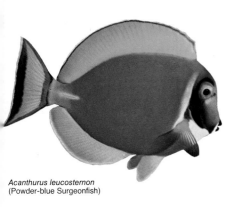

Acanthurus leucosternon
(Powder-blue Surgeonfish)

◄ Some species, for instance surgeonfishes, should not be kept together in one tank with fish of the same family. Also, other fish of the same shape or color are often irritated, sometimes even attacked and injured, so that these species have to be kept apart. These fish, however, can usually live in a community tank with other families without risk or danger.

The beginner, who does not have two tanks, should not start with these species,

even if they are otherwise easily kept. If two aquariums are at hand it is easy to separate two quarrelsome fish from one another.

= Pairs

It is preferable to keep these fish in mated pairs. Only then do they show their best colors and most interesting patterns of behaviour. Even if the sex cannot be determined, it is still advisable to keep them in groups of two. In large tanks – even in community tanks – several pairs of the same species can often be kept together.

Group of Chromis caeruleus (Green Damselfishes)

= Groups

If possible these fish should be kept in groups. Only when three, five or even more fishes are together in one tank do they show their best colors and most interesting patterns of behaviour. Extremely large fish of this type require more room and the aquarist will have to be content with only a few fish. Fish of these species are generally very well-suited for a community tank.

Species which do not have a mark in this column, can be kept singularly, two by two or in larger groups, whichever the hobbyist prefers. It is left to the aquarist how many fishes he wants to keep, according to the space available in his aquarium.

Spotted Scat 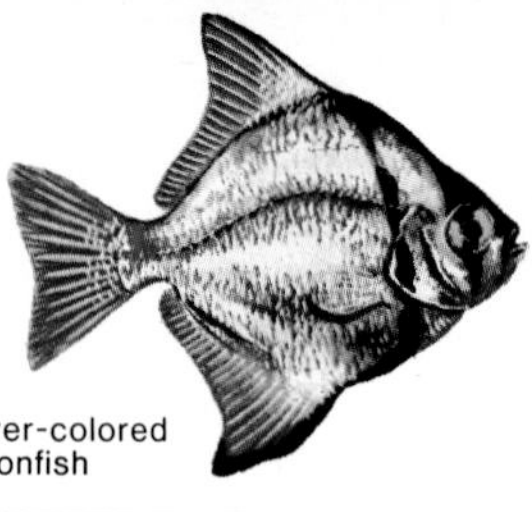   Silver-colored Moonfish

Family		Scientific Name / Popular Name	Amount of Care Required	Native Habitat: Pac. Ind., R.S. Car.	Compatibility	Average Size of Adult Fish inch/cm	Minimum Tank Length inch/cm	TetraMarin,TetraMin T	Tetra Conditioning Food Algae Al, Lettuce Let	Tetra FD-Menu fd / Tetra FD-Food FD	TetraTips	Frozen Food, Fresh Food F F	Artemia
								1	2-3	4-5	6	7-8	9-
Various Families	43	Canthigaster valentini / Sharpnosed Pufferfish	▣	Pac. Ind.	�	6 / 15	24 / 60		Al Let	FD	⌣	F	L
	44	Coris formosa / Yellow-tailed Wrasse	▣	Ind.	⊗	10 / 25	24 / 60	T	⊘	FD ::	⌣	F	A
	45	Coris gaimard / Clown Wrasse	▣	Pac.	⊗	10 / 25	24 / 60	T	⊘	FD ::	⌣	F	A
	46	Elacatinus oceanops / Neon Goby	■	Car.	⊗	2 / 5	20 / 50			::		F	A
	47	Gramma loreto / Royal Gramma	■	Car.	⊗	2 / 6	24 / 60			FD		F	A
	48	Holocentrus rubrum / Squirrelfish	■	Pac. Ind.	⊗	7 / 18	32 / 80			FD	↘	F	
	49	Labroides dimidiatus / Cleanerfish	▣	Pac. Ind.	⊗	4 / 10	24 / 60	T		FD ::	⌣	F	A
	50	Lactoria cornuta / Cowfish	▣	Pac. Ind.	⊸	10 / 25	32 / 80	T		FD	⌣	F	L
	51	Monodactylus argenteus / Moonfish	☐	Pac. Ind.	⊗	6 / 15	32 / 80	T	⊘ Al	fd ::		F	
	52	Myripristis murdjan / Big-eyed Squirrelfish	▣	Pac. Ind. R.S.	⊗	8 / 20	32 / 80			FD	↘	F	L
	53	Odonus niger / Red toothed Triggerfish	■	Pac. Ind.	⊸	12 / 30	40 / 100	T	⊘	FD	⌣	F	
	54	Platax orbicularis / Round Batfish	▣	Pac. Ind.	⊗	16 / 40	40 / 100	T	◉			F	L
	55	Plotosus anguillaris / Saltwater Catfish	▣	Pac. Ind.	⊗	14 / 35	28 / 70	T		FD ::	⌣	F	
	56	Pterois volitans / Lionfish or Turkeyfish	■	Pac. Ind. R.S.	⊗	12 / 30	40 / 100				⌀↘	Heart Liver	Fish L
	57	Rhinecanthus aculeatus / Picasso Triggerfish	▣	Pac. Ind.	⊸	8 / 20	32 / 80		Al Let	FD	⌣	F	
	58	Scatophagus argus / Scat	☐	Pac. Ind.	⊗	6 / 15	32 / 80	T	◉	fd ::	⌣	F	
	59	Thalassoma bifasciatum / Bluehead Wrasse	▣	Car.	⊸	6 / 15	40 / 100	T		FD ::	〖	F	
	60	Zanclus canescens / Moorish Idol	▣	Pac. Ind.	⊸	7 / 18	40 / 100	T	◉ Al Let	FD	〖	F	

Temperature Requirements

All tropical species, mentioned in the table, require water temperatures between 23 and 25° C (73–77° F).

Too low a temperature (under 22° C = 72° F) affects the appetite and facilitates diseases. Too high a temperature may possibly shorten the life of your fish. The most important disadvantage, however, is the lowering of the oxygen content in the water. Warm water retains less oxygen than cool water. Therefore the best average temperature in a salt-water aquarium is 25° C (77° F). The warmer the water is, the more aeration is necessary.

▷◁ = Size of Adult Fish

Indications with regard to size refer to the usual maximum length of the fish to be bought at your dealer's. In their native habitat, salt-water fish often grow to a larger size, but these indications of size would not be useful for the hobbyist. In some particular cases, fish grow more rapidly (in large tanks) than the aquarist prefers. The possible adult size in this case is then indicated in red colour. Fish of such a large size should not be kept at all or only in very large tanks. Otherwise even the best care will only result in cruelty to the fish.

⊢⊣ = Minimum Tank Size

These indications have been proven in practice. In reality, a salt-water aquarium cannot be large enough. On the other hand, the circumstances given and the financial possibilities have to be taken into account.

Tanks below 60 l (16 gal) should only be used for single pairs or for very small fish. For quarantine tanks smaller aquariums are only used when treating few fish.

Never overcrowd your aquarium! The main reason being that a large variety of different species detracts from the attractiveness of each individual fish.

A general rule of thumb for the beginner with regard to the quantity of fish to be kept in an aquarium is the following:

7.5 liters of water for 1 cm of fish or **5 U.S. gal of water for 1 inch of fish.** With regard to species that remain small (under 1½ inch), more fish may be kept, for instance five liters of water for 1 cm of fish or 3.3 U.S. gal of water for 1 inch of fish.

Aeration of the water as well as ozonisation allow the more advanced aquarist to put more fish in an aquarium if biological maintenance of the water quality is guaranteed.

Several Reef Fishes

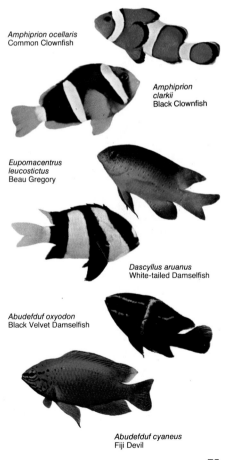

Amphiprion ocellaris
Common Clownfish

Amphiprion clarkii
Black Clownfish

Eupomacentrus leucostictus
Beau Gregory

Dascyllus aruanus
White-tailed Damselfish

Abudefduf oxyodon
Black Velvet Damselfish

Abudefduf cyaneus
Fiji Devil

Foods and the Feeding Plan

The **red** or **bold** type symbols of the feeding plan for instance ▉ indicate that specially favoured food for this fish species is concerned. In some cases the aquarist will find two bold type symbols as both foods are of the same importance. Thin faced type symbols, for instance ⬘ indicate that an additional health promoting food for this species is recommended. Fish species with a **red** symbol need special attention when fed. Red symbols have the same meaning as bold type symbols.

duced, offering all the advantages of the traditional foods. Salt-water fish which are fed on **TetraMarin** do not show signs of deficiency in vitamins. **TetraMin** is a basic

Paracanthurus hepatus (Regal Tang)

food for most seawater fishes today. However, the hobbyist who wants to feed his saltwater fish nearly exclusively with dry food should use **TetraMarin** for the reasons mentioned above. By experience it was ascertained that it is best to use large flakes, because almost all salt-water fish become considerably larger than the smaller species of the freshwater community tank. For smaller salt-water fish the large flakes should be ground up by hand. **TetraMin** and **TetraMarin** are wholesome and easy-to-digest natural flake foods, daily enjoyed by most marine fish.

1. TetraMin or TetraMarin

Compared to **TetraMin, TetraMarin** contains more ingredients of marine origin which, among others, includes algae, kelp, trace elements, and assorted small crustaceans. Due to the balanced and nutritious formula and additional enrichments, the content of vitamins and other nutrients has been raised considerably. For the first time a salt-water fish food had been pro-

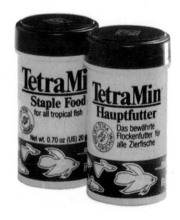

2. Tetra Conditioning Food 🍃∅

Tetra Conditioning Food is produced from a vegetable base. With this food the salt-water aquarist may easily dispense an exact dose of algae food to such fish as surgeonfish, angelfish, and other species that live on a vegetable diet.

Tetra Conditioning Food Large Flakes 🍃∅

The large flakes of **Tetra Conditioning Food** are an excellent replacement for the green algae required by many herbivorous fish. This food is highly recommended for larger fish in excess of 3 inches.

The low protein content found in plants yields a healthy and balanced diet. **Tetra Conditioning Food** large flakes are a beneficial treat for non-plant eating fish as well. Regular feeding will prevent overloading the liver and digestive system thereby eliminating many harmful aspects of overfeeding.

3. **Algae, Lettuce** Al, Al, Let

Many salt-water fish like algae foods such as green algae. Some species prefer *Caulerpa.* Surgeonfish, some chaetodonts, and *Zanclus cornutus* grow better with additional algae food than when exclusively fed with dry food.

What constitutes the value of algae? Apart from the fact that tiny animal organisms live in them and are eaten by fish, they have (as does live food) one inestimable advantage: They are always at the disposal of the fish whenever they are hungry. With regard to salt-water fish this is the case most often the time. In nature, these algae eaters always "graze" on kelp or algae-covered stones. Everything which is a food is then eaten. For one single surgeonfish of about 15 cm (6 inch) length at least a 250 l (66.2 U.S. gal) tank and sufficient decoration are required in order to have a sufficient growth of algae. A tank of this size will usually hardly be at the disposal of most of the hobbyists. However, the need for algae foods cannot be satisfied like this but must be supplemented with other plant-based foods.

After they have been accustomed to it, the species mentioned like fresh scalded head lettuce, too. The same applies to spinach (baby food).

4. Tetra FD-Menu ⠿

The universally nutritious formula contains a great variety of freeze-dried substances such as mosquito larvae, *Tubifex*, liver, heart, and fully grown brineshrimp. Because of the fine screening process, **Tetra FD-Menu** is especially suited for smaller salt-water fish (up to 4 cm [2 inch.] in length). The four separate compartments of the **Tetra FD-Menu** can offer the possibility to regulate the diet by using one of the four special recipes in FD-Menu at a time. Every day or for every feeding the hobbyist may use a different food from one of the four compartments of the can.

Holocanthus (Angelichthys) ciliaris (Queen Angelfish) nibbling at TetraTips

5. Tetra FD Blood Worms ⠿

A basic ingredient from **Tetra FD-Menu** has been separately put on the market by **Tetra: FD Blood Worms.** Almost all chaetodonts accept this food when offered in a tank, even if no other dry food has been accepted before. Fish accept **Tetra FD Blood Worms** as food because of the worm-like shape, which remains even after freeze-drying. By using the method of freeze-drying neither the flavor nor the valuable ingredients are destroyed.

In order to avoid signs of deficiency when feeding **Tetra FD Blood Worms** exclusively during a longer period, the aquarist should offer other food alternatively.

6. TetraTips

This is the right food for fish with strong jaws. Especially triggerfish, angelfish, soldierfish, pufferfish, and many butterflyfish as well as groupers prefer **TetraTips.** Larger species eat one quarter, one half or even one whole tablet. Due to the high vitamin content, fish really enjoy **TetraTips** as a main diet. Many of them do not even need additional live foods. Small fish nibble at **TetraTips.** The contents of this highly nutritional food corresponds approximately to **Tetra FD-Menu.** Anemones and crabs etc. like **TetraTips** as well. Ground up **TetraTips,** soaked in water, are outstanding for living corals. Coral polyps were kept for years when fed **TetraTips,** which proves the high nutritious value of this food.

Significance of the symbols:

⟦⌐ **TetraTips** as valuable additional food or treat food, fastened to the glass ⟦ on the bottom of the tank ⌐ or both ways ⟦⌐.

❲⌐ **TetraTips** are specially favoured, they may serve as main diet.
Way of feeding: see above.

These symbols indicate that in most of the cases **TetraTips** are caught when they are sinking down. Once on the bottom of the tank, these species accept **TetraTips** after some time of adaption only.

7. Frozen Food F F

The most simple way of maintaining fresh food reserves can be done in the refrigerator. Protein foods remain fresh for 1–3 days at temperatures around 0° C (32° F). A deep-freezer with temperatures under −20° C (−4° F) makes it possible to store foods for a longer period of time (up to 2 years). The aquarist has an advantage by this possibility. Quite a number of aquarists can buy live foods, such as adult brine shrimp (especially good), *Daphnia,* blood worms, *Mysis* (not available in U.S.A.) in frozen state at larger pet shops and stock them afterwards in their own deep-freezer. Sea mussels, heart, and liver of beef as well as fish can be frozen (if possible, in feeding portions) as a readily available food.

Algae scraped away when cleaning your aquarium can also be used this way, however, only green algae are suitable.

The feeding and even more the preparing of deep-frozen foods might prove difficult for the hobbyist. Therefore, he often seeks a modern fish food which is easily preserved: by freeze-drying (see under 4 and 5).

8. Sea Mussels, Fish,
Liver and Heart of Beef (Fresh Food)

It is advisable to use only fresh substances. It is practical to freeze the food slightly, to cut it afterwards into portions (approximately the size of a cut pencil) and to use it at once or to deep-freeze it.

The foods mentioned are well-suited for large salt-water fish, but the preparation requires some work.

In order to entice the fish, place the food on the end of a wire or a sharpened wooden stick and move it slightly to and fro in front of the fish's mouth.

For those fish which would not accept any other food than mussels and snails, it is recommended to offer mussels in a clam. The following method is rather complicated but very often successful. The aquarist prepares a pulp, consisting of **TetraMarin**, sea mussels or beef heart. This pulp is spread on a stone, shell or coral. After that the object is dried for approximately 10 minutes in an oven at a temperature of about 70° C (125° F). After drying this "feeding stone" is placed into the aquarium. Butterflyfish, long nosed butterflyfish, angelfish *(Centropyge),* and other finicky eaters like food of this kind. The "feeding stone" should be removed after 20 minutes.

The food is suited for the algae eater as well when mixed with spinach, **Tetra Conditioning Food** or lettuce.

9. Artemia

The durable eggs of brine shrimps *(Artemia salina)* can be bought by the hobbyist in any quantities he needs at most pet shops. Newly hatched nauplii are well-liked by all smaller salt-water fish.

Artemia eggs are tiny: 240,000 of them weigh approximately one gram. Within 36 hours a nourishing live food can be obtained. The hatching of *Artemia* in a culture device is simple.

Artemia Culturing Device

With some difficulty it is possible to even obtain fully-grown crustaceans from *Artemia* eggs. As adults they have a length of 8–10 mm (¼–⅓ inch) then. After reaching this size they are a valuable supplemental food for even larger salt-water fish. At his dealer the aquarist can choose among several devices which will make the hatching of *Artemia* easier.

In comparison to all other substitutes *Artemia* have the advantage of being able to live in salt-water. In this way, they are a

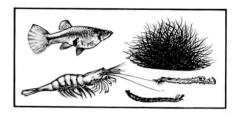

Adult male of the Brine Shrimp *(Artemia salina)* enlarged from 10 mm to 100 mm

"food stock" which remains at the disposal of the fish for a long period of time. Artemia's own movements in the tank entice the fish to snap at them.

As a basic diet, *Artemia* nauplii are not sufficient in the long run because they lack some vitamins and trace elements, as well as amino acids which are of vital necessity for marine fish.

The hobbyist who wants to take the trouble of culturing *Artemia* should feed them finely pulverized **Tetra Conditioning Food.** This food contains the necessary ingredients that fish require. In this form *Artemia* is best suited as a valuable fish food because of the **Tetra Conditioning Food** ingredients with which their intestines are filled.

It is recommended to stop the filter system (but not the bottom filter) during the feeding process and at least 30 minutes after. Like this the aquarist avoids "sucking off" of the brine shrimps.

10. **Live fcod** L L

Food, the way fish find it in nature, is not a practical food source for us. Who could import plankton, worms, snails, and living coral polyps only for this use and keep them alive? Because of these difficulties all live food has to be regarded as a substitute. The most important are:

Mysis or Small Shrimps, e. g. Adult Brine Shrimp

These small crustaceans require large amounts of oxygen. For this reason it is not easy to keep them alive for extended periods of time. Dead crustaceans should not be used as food. In case there should not be a cool place for keeping them the crustaceans could be frozen alive.

Small crustaceans are the best live food for marine fish. There are some difficult species which can only be adapted to tank life by feeding them live food. If the aquarist is not sure to be able to obtain these foods regularly he should refrain from buying difficult fish species.

Enchytraeid Worms

It is easy to breed these white little worms (approx. 10–20 mm = 1/4–3/4 inch long) in small boxes filled with loose soil and placed it in a cool environment. They are greatly sought after as a supplementary food. It is, however, of disadvantage, to use them too often as these worms contain a high amount of fat and after some weeks the fish show signs of malnutrition. In salt-waer enchytreids can stay alive up to two days. They are a good supplementary food for all fish between 2 and 5 inch of length.

Earthworms

Larger fish like small red earthworms. For certain species they are an excellent food, especially in view of their high nutritional value.

Tubifex

These have a high protein value. In salt-water they do not live longer than a few minutes. They burrow under the surface of the sand in an aquarium and die there. Therefore, the aquarist should offer only small portions and observe the feeding closely. To place Tubifex on a plate in order to avoid their burrowing is not of great use as eager fish wash them onto the sand with violent movements of their fins.

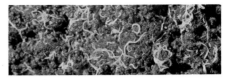

Enchytraeids

Living Tubifex should only be used in case of emergency if no other food is at the disposal of the hobbyist.

Living Fish, Mussels

Some salt-water aquarists breed guppies, as food for young marine fish. However, this kind of feeding should be restricted to exceptions (for instance, lionfish).

A good replacement-food for fussy eaters are mussels in the shell. In many places of the world you can by live "Black mussels" in the shell. Crack the shell end offer this excellent food to your delicate fish.

A typical sea-water aquarium. Only an advanced aquarist will be successful in obtaining a balanced relationship between fish and invertebrates as shown in this picture.

The "Golden Rules"
for the Marine Aquarist

1. Start with easy to handle fish species. Get familiar to their pattern of behaviour in order to recognize deviations at once.

2. Do not start with more than 1 cm of fish for 7.5 liters of water (5 U.S. gal of water for 1 inch of fish).

3. Pay attention to the compatibility of fish. Apart from that it is important that the feeding requirements of the different species coincide.

4. Always provide good aeration and filtration.

5. **Use TetraMarin Large Flakes as a basic diet.** Try to establish the appropriate feeding quantity. Feed very sparingly during the first four weeks. This applies to your show tank as well as to your quarantine tank.

6. A weekly control of density: 1.020–1.024 is recommended; pH-value and nitrite content of the water has to be checked every two weeks.

7. New fish should be put into the quarantine tank first. In case, no quarantine tank is at hand, the entire water quantity of the aquarium may have to be changed after a treatment with medication. Furthermore the filter material as well as the bottom should be carefully cleaned, as the bacteria living there, may have been destroyed by the medication.

8. Never put uncleaned coral-skeletons into your salt-water aquarium. They might contain protein which will foul the water within 24 hours. In such a case there is only one thing to do: for 20 minutes put the fish into fresh salt-water, to which **AquaSafe** has been added in a concentration that is 3–5 times as high as indicated (in case no aged salt-water is at hand). After this time insert the fish into aged salt-water of another tank, or into fresh salt-water with a one to twofold dose of **Aqua-Safe.**

9. **At least every four weeks** ¼ or ⅓ of the water quantity has to be changed. If the tank contains many fish, this has to be done more often. **A regular water change is the secret of a successful marine hobbyist!**

10. When cleaning the filter material of the outside filter, salt-water has to be used always. Fresh tap-water would destroy useful bacteria cultures.

11. Care for the growth of green algae. No medication should be used in the show tank. Change water at regular intervals. Provide sufficient light.

12. Use a good sea salt when preparing new water. Always have a sufficient amount of sea salt in stock.

13. Never catch your fish with a net. Use glass containers into which the fish are gently driven with help of the net. Otherwise the delicate fish skin might be injured.

14. Always have at least the following products in stock:

TetraTest pH "High Range"
TetraTest Nitrite
Tetra AquaSafe
A Copper Remedy for Oodinium and White Spot Disease

Maintenance of the Tank

Cleaning And Water Changes

Because there are no plants in the marine tank it is easier to clean than a freshwater aquarium. Weekly or other cleaning operations should be carried out according to the following points:

1. Clean the covers and light fixtures. Salty covers are easily cleaned under running tap water with the help of an algae scraper and modern cleaning liquids until they are clean. Rinse well and dry.
2. Switch off the filter, air pump, and heater (remove wall plugs). Check nitrite value.
3. Front and side glasses should be cleaned from inside first with an algae scraper. Even the stainless steel blades of the algae scraper should be carefully washed in freshwater afterwards. When working inside the tank the blades of the scraper should be handled with care. Be careful not to damage the silicone seal in the corners of your tank. Be careful that no sand is picked up during the cleaning process, because it might damage even the best glass. Even when using a so-called algae magnet for cleaning the tank glass, the aquarist should be careful that no sand gets betwen the magnet and the glass. If the magnet slips away on the inside of the tank, the aquarist should avoid getting it back by "jiggling" it. The inside magnet should be removed from the tank and the cleaning pad carefully rinsed, then the cleaning can be continued. The inner magnet should not remain in the tank but always be removed after tank cleaning.
4. Corals, stones, etc., should be removed from the aquarium and cleaned in a bucket of salt water from the tank; if necessary, this decorative material should be cleaned with a brush. Do not use freshwater as this would kill algae and microorganisms. Never use detergents in a saltwater tank!

Tetra Hydro-Clean 20/4
The Aquarium Gravel Washer

- Removes dirt and debris
- Siphons 20 gallons in 4 minutes
- Easy starting siphon
- Maximizes under-gravel and power filtration
- Does not disturb decorations

No aquarium is cleaned unless it's Hydro-cleaned

No aquarium is cleaned unless it's Hydro-cleaned

5. Dirt particles should be allowed to sink to the bottom of the tank where they should be removed with a siphon. This has to be done only every 2–3 months, depending on the strength of the filter. During a weekly cleaning, dirt particles can be removed from the tank with a bottom siphon.
6. Thermostatic heater, ozonizer, and filter tubes have to be removed from the tank before they can be cleaned.
7. With a finger or a plastic rod, the aquarist should slightly rake the upper layer of substratum. This avoids a fouling of the bottom material and ensures that the bottom bacteria receive more oxygen.
8. The outside filter should be cleaned every 4–6 weeks; wash the filter material only with saltwater, otherwise the useful bacteria will be killed. If the filter material should smell foul or be so dirty that it cannot be used again, the aquarist should replace it.

This new filter material should be innoculated by adding a handful of the old, unwashed filter material. Highflow filters have to be cleaned more frequently, at least once a week, and the filter material, either diatomaceous earth or synthetic wool, should then be replaced.

9. Decorative material, technical equipment, etc. should be put back into the tank in reverse of the order taken out.
10. Siphoned-off water should be thrown away; fresh saltwater should be added to the tank. Contrary to popular belief, aged saltwater need not be used when making partial water changes. If the tap water is safe, the proper amount of sea salt should be put into a bucket which is then filled with lukewarm tap water and continuously stirred until the proper specific gravity is reached. **AquaSafe** is then added (2 ml/1 U.S. gal [5 ml/10 litre]) and this fresh solution, which is not dangerous to fish, can be poured into the tank. In a show tank, **AquaSafe** should be applied only when no copper treatment has taken place or is scheduled. Check the water density (1.020–1.024); check pH-value.
11. Put the cover on.
12. Tank glasses should be cleaned from the outside with a glass cleaning liquid (but be careful to avoid a drop of this liquid entering the tank) and a newspaper or paper towel.

Daily Checklist
For The Marine Aquarist

1. The lighting should be carefully switched on. Try to avoid startling your fish.
2. Check whether all fish have a healthy appearance (remove any dead fish at once). Check the gill movements of your fish; they should not be too rapid.
3. Check whether airstone and filter work properly.
4. Empty protein skimmer if necessary.
5. Get acquainted with your tank inhabitants so you will notice at once if one of them is missing. Search immediarely: it might be lying in a hidden corner or perhaps even dead.
6. Feed your fish in the morning, at noon (if possible), and in the evening. If no feeding at noon is possible then two morning and evening feeding should be given in-

stead. Do not feed your fish within half an hour before switching off the illumination.

7. Uneaten food, especially larger morsels, should be removed with a net, a plastic dip tube or a wooden stick.
8. Always check the function of the filter and airstone before switching off the illumination. Count your fish, too!
9. When turning off the aquarium lights, the hobbyist should avoid startling the fish by sudden darkness. Another light source in the same room is very practical as it adds dim light to the tank: fish are then able to find their hiding places. Dimmers that make a slow darkening possible prevent shocks to the fish when the illumination is switched on or off.

Your Vacation
and the Marine Tank

There are people who do not buy a marine tank because of possible difficulties when it comes to vacations. Such worries are usually unfounded. Over a weekend (2–3 days total) they can go hungry. The water temperature, however, should be lowered by 4–7° F (2–3° C) to 71–73° F (22–23° C) for the duration of your absence.

During a 3–4 week vacation, however, your fish will have to be fed. Species that are easily kept can be fed flake food with the help of an automatic feeder. More delicate species that require living food or other substitutes need proper feeding at least three times a week. With good will (and a little money!) it is easy to find someone who will do this. Ask your pet shop dealer in case you cannot find anyone. He can usually solve the problem for you.

Four to six weeks before your vacation starts no new fish should be bought in order to diminish the risk of diseases developing in the marine tank while you are away. Only completely healthy fish will survive when cared for by another person.

Prepare the feeding portions (food quantity for one day to be given at one feeding) in advance. Take care that an overfeeding is not possible. Your feeding methods should

Two banner fish *(Heniochus acuminatus)* glide at a depth of 15 m (40 feet) in the Red Sea.

be explained in detail to the volunteer! Have him feed your fish some days before you leave and explain to him the habits of the tank inhabitants, the necessity of checking the temperature, etc. Leave him the address of the nearby pet shop or aquarist friend, thus enabling him to contact these persons in an emergency.

While you are on vacation the illumination should be kept switched on during the hours the fish are accustomed to it. This can be accomplished with a timer switch. Otherwise, this has to be done manually unless the tank receives sufficient illumination by natural daylight. In any case, annual holidays should not prevent the hobbyist from setting up a marine tank.

Diseases –
Their Recognition and Treatment

Diseases are by far the most serious enemy of any marine aquarist. The novice often does not recognize the first stages and misses the best chance for effecting a cure.

A reputable dealer will sell only those fish that have been in a quarantine tank for at least 2–3 weeks. Do not be angry with him if diseases attack your fish anyway. There are diseases that are always present and they manifest themselves only when the specimen is weakened if kept under poor conditions. In newly prepared tanks, tropical marine diseases may spread suddenly. Nearly every newly imported fish is diseased in some way. Most of the time these fish are weakened due to transportation and temperature differences of 10–15°F (6–8°C) or more, and all this within a few hours. Nevertheless, fish survive, but the damage may be so intense that they become sick, especially in their new surroundings.

Fish are infected by various parasites in nature also. However, due to the nearly optimal state of health and the far more remote chance for a parasite to find a new host, the danger for the fish is not so great. But in the confines of a tank, every parasite finds a new host in which it can live. Hence, diseases are more of a problem here.

The aquarist should practice recognizing fish diseases and their symptoms. Ask your dealer and friends to show you dis-eased fish and have them explain the best methods of recognition and treatment.

Start with a few inexpensive fish and keep them for some weeks. If these particular specimens continue to be healthy, and eat properly, you can purchase more delicate species. The aquarist should never forget, however, to keep newcomers in a quarantine tank for at least 3 weeks. Otherwise he runs the risk of infecting the established tank inhabitants.

The hobbyist who cannot restrain himself from spending large sums of money on fish right from the start can be sure it will be expensive setting up a marine tank. Expensive fish are often more delicate (that's why they are so expensive) and often more susceptible to disease than less expensive specimens. Use your common sense! It is a great pleasure to buy more beautiful and delicate fish after easier species have been successfully kept. The Care and Feeding Table will inform you of the "degrees of difficulty" for the different species of fish.

In spite of caution and care, the novice aquarist might still experience losses due to disease in the marine tank. It is therefore recommended to stick closely to the following rules:

1. Every symptom should be taken seriously. The following factors have to be checked: pH and nitrite value, specific gravity, temperature and color of the water. For safety's sake, $1/3$ of the tank water should be replaced with fresh saltwater on a regular basis.

2. If one fish is diseased, others are usually infected also.

3. All fish should be treated in a quarantine tank, not in the show tank. If no second tank is at hand, all fish must then be treated in the show tank. The use of a copper medication in the show tank leads to another danger: the copper will never disappear completely from the tank if the water is not completely changed. The copper precipitates out, and that is why producers of copper medications recommend a second and third treatmend after 2 or 4 days. However, should the pH-value drop,

some of the remaiming copper may redissolve, thus becoming poisonous to the tank inhabitants again. A complete water change is therefore recommended after a copper medication has been used and the disease has been cured. Dead algae have to be removed carefully as they store copper which becomes free again when they decay.

4. Never use more than one medication at a time. In case the first treatment was not successful, at least 3/4 of the tank water should be renewed before a second medication is used.

5. Never put newcomers into the show tank.

6. Feed the fish sparingly when under medication to avoid pollution of the water and a consequent water change and a renewed treatment.

7. If the medication is done in a show tank, the outside filter should be switched off before and during the treatment, until the water has been changed and the medication is finished. If possible, never use a medication in a tank with a biological filter. High flow filters should be switched on.
When switched off, biological outside filters are rendered useless, which means that nitrifying bacteria living in the filter material die because of lack of oxygen. The pumps should therefore be kept switched on and circulated through a bucket or a small tank. Otherwise, the filter material should be renewed.

8. Vigorous aeration has to be provided when the filter is not functioning.

9. Ultraviolet light, the protein skimmer and the ozonizer have to be switched off during medication.

10. After most medications in the show tank a complete renewal of the tank water is necessary. After that the pump of the outside filter may be used again together with a biological filter. It may be put back into use immediately again if it has been kept switched on using a bucket.

11. **MarinOomed** should be kept available all times.

How to Recognize Diseased Fish in Time

For the inexperienced hobbyist the recognition of diseases is one of the most difficult problems he faces.

Symptoms of Disease

If new fish do not eat after two days, something might be wrong with them. Perhaps they are not accustomed to the food or the water conditions. Their rejection of the food may indicate a disease. Later, in a more advanced stage of the disease, they will refuse to eat. Now it is high time to begin a treatment as outlined below.

Another cause for the rejection of food might be damages that occurred because the fish were caught with the help of anaesthetics. Fish that are caught like this usually cannot be saved. They reach the dealer in apparently good condition, but they do not eat. Organs like the liver have been destroyed by the poison with which they were caught. The aquarist can keep such a specimen in his tank for some days or even weeks, until it finally dies – starved to death.

Only buy those fish that eat at your pet shop. Then you can be sure they were not "poisoned". Phillippine law forbids the use of anaesthetics in capturing fish. The problem of acquiring such fish, however, is real.

Apart from the rejection of food there exists another symptom: fish often swim with jerky movements and rub against corals, stones or any other rough surfaces in an effort to scrape off parasites.

A third symptom, easily recognizable for the beginner, is excessive rate of respiration. If the rate of breathing is faster than the aquarist can easily count and there is no lack of oxygen in the tank, there is a strong possibility that the gills have parasites. A low pH-value or a high nitrite value might induce rapid breathing; therefore these values should be checked before making a diagnosis.

The fourth symptom of a parasite attack is hovering in the water stream of the filter outlet or in the rising bubbles of the airstone; the fish find more oxygen here which will ease their gill problems. The main diseases of saltwater fish are the following:

1. *Oodinium ocellatum* (Protozoa) (Coral Fish Disease)
2. *Cryptocarion irritans* (Protozoa) (Dot Disease, Saltwater Ich) Similar to the freshwater *Ichthyophthirius*
3. Gill Worms *(Trematodes)*
4. Skin Fungus *(Fungus)*
5. Fin Rot *(Bacteria)*
6. *Lymphocystis* (Virus) (Tubercle Disease, Knot Disease)

Oodinium (Coral Fish Disease, Marine Velvet)

The most common disease is coral fish disease or *Oodinium,* which attacks the fish in the following areas of the body:

1. In the intestines
2. On the gills
3. On the body and fins

The *Oodinium* cells cannot be seen in the intestines or on the gills. An inexperienced hobbyist may easily recognize grey, white or yellowish pinpoint dots on the body and the fins of his fish.

In particular, tiny dots can be seen on dark and transparent parts of the body. It is advantageous to look at the fish when it swims directly towards the observer or when light enters the tank from above or from the sides. The tiny dots on the fish, which are the parasitic stage, leave the fish as cysts and release free-swimming stages which attack other fish.

It takes 7–10 days for the free swimmers to settle on a new fish and to form a new cyst. This first attack of *Oodinium* is relatively easy to cure. Unfortunately, it is often not recognized soon enough. Further symptoms of *Oodinium* are:

1. When the fins do not open easily
2. When the fish rub against rough objects.

As the infection builds up attack is far more severe.

The experienced hobbyist can see masses of tiny spots on the skin of the fish. Fish rub more frequently and start an abnormal rapid breathing which is due to the parasites attaching themselves to the gill filaments, thus hampering respiration. Even in this critical stage, *Oodinium* can be cured with the medication described below.

If the infection progresses it is very dangerous, or even fatal, for delicate fish. Fish show a yellowish-grey coating of parasite cysts that are lying close together. The eyes of the fish may become dull, the rate of respiration becomes rapid and the fish refuse to eat. At this stage an immediate treatment is necessary! Remember not to treat the fish in the show tank! A separate hospital tank, which should be at least half the size of your show tank is necessary. If no aged saltwater is available, remove some water from the show tank until half of the hospital tank is filled. The remaining half should be filled with fresh tap water. Specific gravity reading: 1.015 and temperature approximately 86° F (30° C). The quarantine tank requires a thermostat-heater. The parasites will die off in the show tank within 5–8 days if there are no fish in it. The most popular and approved remedy against *Oodinium* in saltwater is copper sulphate. The aquarist should apply it in a concentration of around 0.8–1 ppm (parts per million), i.e. 0.8–1 mg per litre of tank water. Stick closely to the directions for use of the various remedies which are available from pet shops.

When using **MarinOomed*** from **Tetra,** fish as well as lower animals may remain in the show tank. An overdose, however, may prove harmful to lower animals (invertebrates) and if they die and decay, fish might be killed also. Fish should preferably be removed as described before and put into the hospital tank, while lower animals may remain in the show tank. **MarinOomed** offers the advantage of a safe application: without a water change, the aquarist may add it to the tank water 3–5 times, with a two day interval between treatments, until the symptom of the coral fish disease have disappeared. After this procedure a water change is necessary.

The aquarist cannot expect to completely eradicate *Oodinium* parasites among his fish, as they can also be found in the fish intestines. The health status of weakened fish can considerably worsen. *Oodinium* inside a fish can hardly be treated. Even

* If MarinOomed is not available at your dealer, use a good copper remedy.

without putting newcomers into the tank, weak specimens might be attacked weeks after the treatment has been completed. This is especially true with new imports, even if these fish have a healthy appearance. The aquarist should provide good water conditions and the proper diet to try and **prevent** the disease.

Life cycle of Oodinium

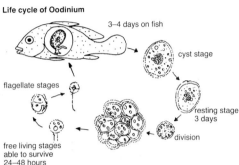

3–4 days on fish

cyst stage

flagellate stages

resting stage
3 days

division

free living stages able to survive 24–48 hours

Amphiprion clarkii with an obvious *Oodinium* infestation.

Cryptocaryon irritans
(Marine "Ich")

The course of this disease is similar to that of *Oodinium* and *Ichthyophthirius;* the freshwater aquarist will already know about this latter disease. The *Cryptocaryon* parasites on the fish's body are easier to recognize than those of *Oodinium*. *Cryptocaryon* manifests itself in whitish pimples about the size of a pinhead. Thus the cysts are considerably larger than those of *Oodinium.* The same symptoms can be ob-

served: fish rub frequently on rough surfaces and the gill movements increase.

A successful treatment with copper sulphate as described above can be used. Do not put the fish back into the show tank immediately after the medication as there may be free-swimming parasites left that will attack the fish. The cysts on the tank bottom die within 24 hours if they do not find a new host.

When using a medication, **all** fish have to be removed from the show tank. In a hospital tank they have to be treated for at least 10 days. After this time the aquarist may transfer them back into their set-up tank. Expecially suited for medication against *Cryptocaryon* is **MarinOomed.**

Life cycle of Cryptocaryon

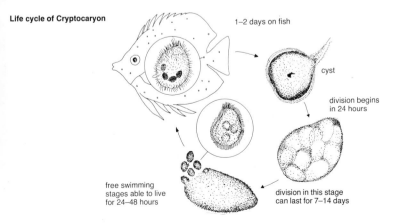

1–2 days on fish

cyst

division begins in 24 hours

division in this stage can last for 7–14 days

free swimming stages able to live for 24–48 hours

Cryptocaryon on the head and fins of a butterfly fish (Forciper longirostris)

Gill Worms (Trematodes)

This is one of the most frequent marine fish diseases and it is most difficult to recognize. Butterfly fish, angelfish, and surgeons are the chief targets. Frequently these worms can be observed with the naked eye.

First the gills are attacked and the parasites can be seen under the gill plates. There are approximately 50 different species of these gill worms but not all of them can be seen with the naked eye. If the gills of a fish are not dark red but show a whitish or pinkish coloration, it is likely that the fish is suffering from a gill parasite infestation. An extremely rapid rate of gill movements (without any noticeable symptoms of the above mentioned two diseases, not including from lack of oxygen, too high temperatures, low pH-value and/or a high nitrite value of the water) indicates almost certainly that the fish are suffering from gill worms.

A treatment with copper sulphate will be inadequate. A rapid and effective method is as follows: The fish should be placed into a freshwater solution, containing 10% saltwater (1 part seawater in 9 parts fresh) at a temperature of 79° F (26° C). Even the most delicate fish sepecies have been treated successfully to this method. They were cured of their gill worms and continued to live even after they had refused food for days and were as thin. Do not be afraid to try this radical cure! However, avoid placing the fish into straight fresh water.

The period of treatment has to be adjusted according to the different fish species: it ranges from 20 minutes to 6 hours. If delicate and expensive fish are involved, the freshwater cure should only be affected if the fish can be observed throughout the treatment. As soon as soon as the patients turn to the side or show signs of discomfort they should be replaced into the saltwater tank. With this method gill worms die because they cannot tolerate the rapid change of salinity. This treatment costs nothing; it may be used repeatedly until your fish are healthy again.

Formalin may also be used to treat gill worms, and details may be found in most fish disease books.

Until now there was little known about the life cycle of gill trematodes. It is, however, relatively certain that these parasites do swim around freely, therefore it is dangerous to place the fish back in the show tank immediately after they have been treated. It is possible that other tank inhabitants are also infected. Since this disease is easily

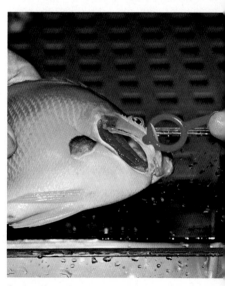

Gently open the gill covers to inspect the gills – they should be a clean, dark red

recognized by the rate of gill movements it is recommended to only treat those fish with the freshwater method that actually show a rapid breathing rate.

Masoten, manufactured by **Chem-Agro.** in the U.S. has been used successfully against gill worms. The dosage is 0.5 ppm (active ingredient) as a long-term bath. Attention! **Masoten** can be dangerous! The slightest overdose may kill your fish immediately. Do not inhale it either!

An approved remedy is **Gyromed*** from **Tetra,** which can even be used in combination with **MarinOomed***, but in quarantine tanks only.

* Neither of these products are available on a world-wide basis. Ask your **Tetra** stockist for details.

Skin Fungus

This can easily be confused with the grey-whitish coating of *Oodinium* parasites. This skin "fungus" results from tiny parasites attacking the skin and the gills of the fish. They perforate the skin, leaving little injuries and then the fungus will invade the fish. Very low temperatures and poor water conditions causing a decay of the outer skin cells of the fish, might be a factor causing fungus infections as well. If no grey dots are recognized even with the help of a magnifying glass, the fish is suffering from fungus, otherwise by *Oodinium.*

First of all, the water has to be checked for the pH level and nitrite content. Most of the time the aquarist will find that a water change is urgently required when fungus is present. For a medication, **Tetra General Tonic** (treatment in a quarantine tank) is recommended. After 5 days the grey skin coating should have disappeared. After the treatment with **General Tonic,** fish may be released into the show tank, where 1/2 to 3/4 (or even more) of the tank contents have been replaced with fresh saltwater.

Amphiprion ocellaris and all species of this family are especially susceptible to fungus; for these popular fish, a 3–5 day treatment with **General Tonic** in a quarantine tank is usually successful.

If a small number of *Amphiprion* are kept with sea anemones, they are only rarely attacked by diseases. A very low pH-value (below pH 8) and a very high nitrite value are the main causes of skin fungus.

Gill Rot

This occurs only rarely in saltwater fish. If it does, it is only in combination with other diseases, usually with skin fungus. Usually the origin of gill rot is poor water quality. Treatment by water change and the application of **Tetra General Tonic** is recommended. A simultaneous and follow-up treatment with **Tetra AquaSafe** improves the regeneration of the fish's skin.

Lymphocystis on a *Scatophagus*

Lymphocystis

The edges of gill plates and fins are most often attacked. From the outer edges the disease spreads inwards so that in an advanced state the entire fin area is covered by knot-like white, gelatinous lumps.

In most cases a medication is of no use. A radical cure has been successful even when delicate species were involved. The attacked fin edges should be trimmed with scissors and then painted with iodine to prevent infection. Iodine should be diluted with **Tetra AquaSafe** (1 part iodine to 3 parts **AquaSafe).** Watch out when handling the gill plates! The solution must never enter the gills or the eyes of the fish. Be careful when holding the fish (use a wet cloth). This treatment is somewhat risky and can only be done with large fish.

Lymphocystis is a contagious viral disease which may affect fish predisposed by poor water conditions. It is known to the freshwater hobbyist as well. Change the tank water regularly and take nitrite/nitrate measurements frequently (every one to two weeks).

After trimming the fins and painting them with iodine, the fish should be transferred back into a tank containing clean salt water. To avoid secondary infections and fungus on fins, **GeneralTonic** and **AquaSafe** should be added to the hospital tank.

I would like to repeat once again: it is very likely that all new fish are infected with parasites. Therefore, I strongly recommend that the aquarist not introduce them into the set-up tank with his established fish, but rather to watch them carefully in a quarantine tank, and if necessary, treat them there.

The water of the hospital tank has to be replaced completely after a treatment to avoid mixing different remedies.

Only when setting up a new aquarium may all specimens be placed into the show tank at once. These fish should be observed very closely during the first 2–4 weeks. In case of diseases they will have to be treated in the show tank. The new hobbyist should apply **MarinOomed** as a prophylatic measure to prevent coral fish disease.

After a medication has been affected in the show tank, a nearly complete water change has to be made. The beneficial natural bacteria may be destroyed for

Skin fungus and fin rot on a *Chromis*. Treatment with **General Tonic** and **AquaSafe** would be recommended.

weeks or even months, as they are often killed by the remedies mentioned.

Copper Poisoning

The new aquarist might have cause to panic after and overdosage of copper remedies. Fish may float on the water surface with their bellies turned up; they might show bent spines or just lie on the bottom of the tank, their breathing rate very slow and showing no reflex movements. They do not react to a net or a hand. These symptoms could indicate nitrite/ammonium poisoning (look for dead fish!). Check the nitrite immediately and then change some of the water; while doing this the fish in question should be revived in a bucket of saltwater treated with **AquaSafe.**

If the concentration of the copper remedy was too high, only a quick reaction by the hobbyist will help in such a case. Water should be taken from the tank and **Aqua Safe** should be added (3–5 times the normal dose) and into which the fish should be placed. Good aeration should also be provided. After 20 minutes the fish should be released into a aquarium where no copper medication has been used. If the hobbyist has only one tank, he should then replace half of its contents with fresh saltwater. Thus the copper concentration will be cut down by 50%.

It is also possible to add **AquaSafe** directly to the hospital tank. In this case, however, only a normal dose should be used. **Aqua Safe** immediately renders the copper ineffective. If a disease still persists, a complete water change has to be made after the **AquaSafe** treatment in order to apply the copper remedy once again. When using **MarinOomed,** copper poisoning is avoided.

The beginnings of lymphocystis on *Angelicthys ciliaris*.

Table of Diseases

The Most Important Diseases and Injuries of Marine Fish in the Aquarium.

Disease	Cause	Symptoms	a) Period of Quarantine b) Infectious c) Length of Treatment	Confirmation	Treatment and Corrective Measures	Dosage and Application
Avitaminosis (lack of vitamins).	Incorrect feeding too much *Tubifex*, enchytraeids.	Holes in gill covers, swollen gills, red veins all over the body, ragged mouth edges, eventually attacked by fungus.	a) Not applicable. b) Not applicable. c) 3–4 weeks.	By observation.	Water change, **TetraRuby** should be offered for 4 weeks; if no flake food is accepted, fluid vitamins should be given in other food or in the water.	Drop fluid vitamins on brine shrimp or scallop flesh.
Cryptocaryon irritans, Salt Water Ich.	Unicellar ciliate protozoans form cysts under or on the fish's skin, releasing a capsule. Within 24 hours this capsule divides on the tank floor. Within the following 8 days up to 200 ciliates develop. They are able to move and search out a new host to live on.	White, pin-sized dots on skin and fins; easily observed on dark parts of the body and transparent fins. Fish rub on the tank bottom and sharp objects.	a) Up to 4 weeks. b) Yes, definitely. c) At least 4 weeks.	Visible to the naked eye. Diameter of cyst approximately $1/2$ mm; diameter of ciliates approximately $1/20$ mm.	1. Copper sulphate: 2.* **MarinOomed:** 3. **Contralck:** 4. Quinine hydrochloride (which will not kill the bacteria in the tank). **Never** apply remedies that contain copper together with **GeneralTonic** and **AquaSafe; AquaSafe** cancels out the effect of copper.	0.8–1 ppm. After a successful medication, $3/4$ of the water should be changed, and algae removed from the tank. Normal dose; afterwards, half the dose every 2–3 days until no more cysts can be found (may take up to 2 weeks). Normal dose, half the dose after 4 days. This remedy is not safe in tanks without a bottom substrate. 1–2 g for 26 U.S. gal (100 l) of tank water. Water change after 2–3 days, to be repeated until a recovery can clearly be seen. Will not kill bacteria in the tank.
Fish Lice (*Argulus)*, many different species.	Attack by lice of 2–5 mm in length.	Roundish wounds, showing red edges, caused by bites.	a) 2 weeks. b) Yes, these parasites move from host to host. c) Not applicable.	Easily seen with the naked eye; serious outbreaks are rare.	Removal with tweezers; disinfection of tank. Can only be affected with remedies that may be harmful to the fish (see **Masoten**). Secondary infection (bacteria and fungus) to be treated with **GeneralTonic.**	**Masoten:** 1:100,000 (1 g per 26 U.S. gal [1 g per 100 l] of tank water), short bath treatment for 15 minutes, to be repeated if necessary. **GeneralTonic.** 1 ml per 2 liters of water.
Skin Fungus (do not mistake for *Oodinium* in *Amphiprion* species).	1. Attack of fungus or bacteria (when in symbiosis with a sea anemone, fish are not attacked). 2. *Gyrodactylus* (small worms). 3. Poor water conditions.	Grey coating of the fish's body, later eyes turn dim.	a) 2 weeks. b) Yes. c) 2–5 days.	*Gyrodactylus* (worm of approximately 1.5 mm in length) can be seen with a microscope and sometimes even with the naked eye.	Water change, **GeneralTonic** and **AquaSafe** should be added.	10 ml/5 U.S. gal (1 ml/2 l) of tank water.

*Note: not available on a worldwide basis.

Disease	Cause	Symptoms	a) Period of Quarantine b) Infectious c) Length of Treatment	Confirmation	Treatment and Corrective Measures	Dosage and Application
Ichthyosporidium *(Ichthyophonus)*. A fungal infection.	Unicellular parasites develop in the stomach and intestines and are discharged with the faeces. Some penetrate the intestines and invade liver, heart and kidneys, where they form capsules. The cysts develop, then divide several times, damaging the host organ so that the fish dies. An infection may be carried by copepods which may invade a marine tank. Usually fish with this disease have already been sick in their native habitat. Poor water conditions help this disease to spread.	Skin and scales are rough as sandpaper. Later the fish turn around on their own axis in a rocking motion. Sometimes abcesses form and the skin bursts open. Loss in weight, the skin becomes pale; fins open. Mouth continuously open. Fish may die after about 6 months.	a) Useless! b) Possibly. c) Incurable!	Only with the help of a microscope by a pathologist after the death of the fish (small dark stains in liver, heart or kidneys).	A recovery is seldom possible. An increase in resistance is obtained by offering vitamins as well as food of good quality (**TetraMarin** and **TetraRuby**). Remove fish that seem to be diseased and kill them if they do not recover visibly.	3–4 feedings daily.
Gill Maggots	Coepods of the genus *Ergasilus*, 0.2–2.0 mm in length. The pincers of these crustaceuns attack the gills.	When lifting up the gill plates, small white animals are to be seen; especially visible are the grey-brown egg tubes lying between the red gill filaments. At a later stage the gills turn pink.	a) Not necessary, unless attack is easily visible. b) Possibly. c) 1 week.	With the naked eye, or according to the species, only detectable with a microscope.	1. **Masoten:** 2. Potassium permanganate. 3. Formalin	1:100,000 for 15 minutes. 1 g per 2.6 U.S. gal. (10 l) of water. 1 ml (35–40% strength) per quart (1 l) of water for 10 minutes. Aerate during treatment.
Gill Trematodes *(Benedenia melleni)*. There exist approximately a dozen different species.	Parasite, laying eggs from which free-swimming larva develop after 8 days, which attack new fish within approximately 6 hours.	Gills are attacked, open wounds; fish lose their scales; secondary attack by bacteria.	a) 10 days. b) Yes. c) 8 days.	Lift up the gill plate which should show a bloody red color if the fish is healthy. A pink coloration may indicate a gill fluke attack. Larvae are 0.2 mm in length; adult approximately 4 mm; easily visible with the naked eye. Some species are smaller.	Freshwater treatment for 15 minutes. Temperature should be the same as in the show tank. The salinity change is harmful to the worms, while marine fish can tolerante it more easily. Bacterial attack should be treated with **GeneralTonic**. **Masoten:**	0.5 g/260 U.S. gal (1000 l) of water. Attention, this remedy is only tolerated by some fish.

Disease	Cause	Symptoms	a) Period of Quarantine b) Infectious c) Length of Treatment	Confirmation	Treatment and Corrective Measures	Dosage and Application
Lymphocystis	This virus attacks skin and fins, mostly on the edges. These white, abcess-like thickenings are caused by reactions of the fish's skin.	White, knot-like thickenings on the fins and edges of the gill plates and mouth, later to be found all over the fish's body. The secondary attack of bacteria is additionally harmful to the fish.	a) None, if no attack is seen. b) Yes, but rarely. c) Several weeks, until a complete recovery has been obtained.	Attacks are easily visible with the naked eye.	The specific gravity should be lowered to 1.015 for one week. Ozonization and ultraviolet light should be used to stop secondary infections. Fin edges should be trimmed, afterwards painted with iodine and **Aqua-Safe.** Water conditions should be improved and **GeneralTonic** added.	1 part of iodine and 2 parts **AquaSafe** for painting. **GeneralTonic:** 2 ml per 1 U.S. gal (1 ml per 2 l) of tank water.
Oodinium ocellatum, Coral Fish Disease.	Dinoflagelates, attacking the fish's skin and fins. After 3–4 days approximately 256 free-swimming spores are released which seek out a new host. *Oodinium ocellatum* is easily and successfully treated in the free swimming stage.	The fish's mouth is open, the gill plates are spread open. Increased rate of respiration. Fish remain in the bubbles of the airstone or in the water stream of the filter output. Dark skin shows a velvet-like cover if the fish is seriously attacked. Whitish-yellowish or grey dots (which can only be seen with a magnifying glass) cover the different parts of the body. Fish rub and refuse to eat.	a) At least 10 days. b) Yes, very! c) 15 days, as these parasites are found in the intestines as well, where they cannot be treated. It is therefore recommended to keep diseased fish in quarantine tank for another 10 days after a complete recovery has taken place.	Tiny dots or yellowish-grey coloration seen on skin and fins. At a later stage the fish looks as if sugar powdered. Diameter of the cyst $^1/_{20}$ mm. It is thus recommended to use a magnifying glass or, even better, a microscope.	Copper sulphate: Quinine hydrochloride: **MarinOomed:**	0.8–1 ppm. After a recovery has taken place. $^3/_4$ of the water should be renewed. Tank should be cleaned of algae. 1–2 g/26 U.S. gal (100 l) of tank water. Water change after 2–3 days. To be repeated until a recovery is clearly seen. 2 ml per 3 U.S. gal (12 l) of tank water. To be repeated (half the dose) every 48 hours until no more symptoms are visible.
Fungus	Wounds, caused by copepods, *Dactylogyrus*, and *Gyrodactylus*. The edges of the wounds are attacked by fungus.	Secondary, cotton wool-like infection of the wounds.	a) Not applicable. b) Yes. c) 10 days.	Visible; cotton wool-like infection of the wounds.	Water quality should be improved (partial water change); addition of **GeneralTonic** and **AquaSafe.**	2 ml per 1 U.S. gal (1 ml per 2 l) of tank water.
Diarrhoea.	Unbalanced diet too cool deep-frozen food (not thawed out!). Overfeeding.	No food is accepted, swollen body, no interest in eating, spiting out food.	a) Not applicable. b) Not applicable. c) 2–8 days.	By observation.	Freshwater treatment, water change, adding a double dose of **AquaSafe.** No feedings for 2–3 days. Algae should be offered if the fish in question is an algae eater. In a critical situation castor oil to be dropped into the fish's mouth.	**AquaSafe:** 2 ml per 1 U.S. gal (1 ml per 2 l) of water. Castor oil: 1–2 drops per fish.

Disease	Cause	Symptoms	a) Period of Quarantine b) Infectious c) Length of Treatment	Confirmation	Treatment and Corrective Measures	Dosage and Application
Poisoning: 1. Metal Poisoning. 2. Nitrite/Nitrate Poisoning. 3. Chemical Poisoning. 4. Puffer Fish Poisoning. 5. Hydrogen Sulphide Poisoning.	1. Objects in the tank containing copper, zinc, or metal trace elements (e.g. stones). Usually, however, due to an overdose of copper remedies, hot water heaters and water pipes made of copper. 2. Overfeeding, overcrowding, new tank, not yet biologically active. 3. Hair spray or insecticides, remains of washing agents (detergents) in the bucket used for water change. 4. Puffer fish might release a poisonous substance when killed or startled, which might kill the rest of the tank inhabitants. It is therefore recommended that the novice refrains from keeping this fish. 5. Rotten tank bottom, filter not functioning.	1–3: Dim, dull eyes, heavy breathing, restlessness and later whirling about. When reaching the final stages fish will lie on the tank bottom or the water surface and no longer react to stimuli. 4–5: Dim eyes, heavy breathing; delicate species die within a short period of time. The remaining tank inhabitants can only be saved by taking them out of the tank immediately.	a) Not applicable. b) Not applicable. c) From 20 minutes up to some days.	1–2. By a copper or NO₂-N test, the aquarist should check the cause of the poisoning. If no result is obtained it is recommended to check whether some sort of spray was used near the tank. 3. The Puffer Fish poisoning cannot be specifically identified. 4. Hydrogen sulphide poisoning should be checked by a smelling the tank bottom and filter material. Penetrating smell of sulphur (like rotton eggs) indicates sulphur poisoning.	1–3. Water change during which distressed fish should be placed in a bucket with fresh saltwater, to which a double dose of Aqua-Safe has been added. The aquarist should provide good aeration. A well-prepared hospital tank is best, if not already occupied by diseased fish. 4. Incurable. Sometimes an immediate replacement with new saltwater to which AquaSafe has been added, will help if the poisoning has not lasted too long. 5. Tank bottom and filter material should be replaced. ³⁄₄ of the water has to be changed. AquaSafe has to be added.	1–3. **AquaSafe** 4 ml/U.S. gal (1 ml/1 l) of tank water for a treatment in the bucket. 4–5. **AquaSafe** 4 ml/U.S. gal (1 ml/1 l) of water.
Vibrio anguillarium, Ulcer Disease	Bacteria attack by *Vibrio anguillarium* can be caused by temperature changes, overcrowded tanks, bad food, wounds incurred on the transport (when catching the fish with a net instead of using a glass container).	No appetite, discoloration of skin, fin rot, later open wounds and abcesses, redness of the vent and fin edges.	a) 8 days. b) Under poor conditions, yes. Otherwise, seldom. c) 7 days.	Only for ichthyologists with the aid of a microscope.	The bad conditions have to be corrected. **GeneralTonic** and **AquaSafe** should be added. In critical cases chloramphenicol should be given in a treatment tank, ½ of this water should be changed every 2 days (re-treatment necessary).	**GeneralTonic:** 2 ml/U.S. gal (1 ml/2 l) of water. Chloramphenicol: 50 mg/U.S. gal (13 mg/1 l) of tank water.
Wounds	External injuries due to the use of a net. Wounds caused by rowdy tank mates. Crustacean parasites. Abcesses bursting open.	Wounds to be seen on fins, skin and gills, showing pink coloration. Usually the caudal fin is especially attacked. Wounds may be caused by gill maggots and fish lice as well as internal organ diseases, for instance *Ichthyophonus.*	a) 3–8 days. b) Not applicable. c) 3–8 days.	Can be seen externally.	Diseased fish should be separated and put into fresh saltwater to which **AquaSafe** and **GeneralTonic** have been added. Feed sparingly, wounds should be painted with iodine and **AquaSafe.**	**GeneralTonic:** 2 ml/U.S. gal (1 ml/2 l) of water. **AquaSafe:** 2 ml/U.S. gal (1 ml/2 l) of water. Iodine: 1 part of iodine to be diluted with 3 parts of **AquaSafe.**

Important – never use any chemicals with invertebrates present unless you **know** that it is safe.

Useful Literature and Addresses

I. Other books by **Tetra Press:**

Beginners Aquarium Digest by Dr. U. Baensch / H. A. Baensch (1975)
Marine Care and Feeding Table by H. A. Baensch (1975)
Tropical Aquarium Fish by Dr. U. Baensch (1983)
Coldwater Fish in the Home and Garden by Prof. W. Ladiges (1983)

Ask at your **Tetra** stockist for details.

II. Other useful books:

Saltwater Aquarium Fish by H. R. Axelrod/W. E. Burgess (T.F.H., 1973)
Marine Tropical Aquarium Guide by Frank de Graaf (T.F.H.,1982)
Marine Aquarium Keeping by S. Spotte (Wiley Interscience, 1973)
Brackish Aquariums by M. W. Gos (T.F.H., 1979)
Diseases of Marine Aquarium Fishes by M. P. Dulin (T.F.H., 1976)

III. Useful addresses:

International Marine Aquarium Society
c/o James DeBernado
91, Tulip Avenue, Fc. 2, Floral Park, NY 1101, U.S.A.

British Marine Aquarists Association
c/o Steve Preston, 16, Fountain Drive, Child Lane,
Liversedge, West Yorks., V. K.

IV. Magazines:

Aquarium Digest International, Tetra Sales (U.S.A.)
201, Tabor Road, Morris Plains, New Jersey, 07950. U.S.A.

or

c/o Tetra Information Centre
15, Newlay Lane Place, Leeds. LS13 2BB, Yorkshire. UK.

Tropical Fish Hobbyist Magazine, T. F. H. Publications Inc.
211, W. Sylvania Avenue, Neptune City, New Jersey, 07753. U.S.A.

or

c/o T. F. H. Publications Ltd.
11, Ormside Way, Holmethorpe Industrial Estate, Redhill RHI 2 PX. UK.

Aquarist and Pondkeeper
The Buckley Press, The Butts, Hall Acre, Brentford, Middlesex. UK.

Practical Fishkeeping
EMAP National Publications, Bretton Court, Bretton, Peterborough. UK.

Freshwater and Marine Aquaria
120, West Sierra Madre Boulevard, Sierra Madre, California. 91024. U.S.A.

Index to Fish Scientific Names

Photographs:

Peter Chlupaty, Milan Chvojka, Prof. Dr. Hans W. Fricke, Hilmar Hansen, Ulrich Heinemann, Burkard Kahl, Horst Kipper, Hans-Jürgen Mayland, Arend van den Nieuwenhuizen, Gerhard Siepmann, Hans A. Baensch (author), Tetra-Archiv

Illustrations:

B. Kahl, Angela Paysan, Tetra-Archiv